PASTORAL
CARE
IN THE
LIBERAL
CHURCHES

PASTORAL CARE IN THE LIBERAL CHURCHES

Edited by
James Luther Adams
and
Seward Hiltner

ABINGDON PRESS
Nashville and New York

For
Jeanne Wennerstrom
Ann Wennerstrom
Eric Wennerstrom

May this book bring sharpened memory of a husband and father who had insight, courage, and compassion—and who deeply loved his family

CONTENTS

FOREWORD

The archeologist does not depend primarily upon the work of the earthworm, but he is grateful for its tireless assistance. The earth is inhabited by billions of earthworms, eating their way relentlessly through the subsoil. By this ceaseless activity they loosen the soil around movable objects so that gradually these objects rise to the surface. As a consequence the farmer is again and again obliged to clear away the stones and other objects that emerge into sight. Similarly the archeologist, even without digging, finds on the surface cultural artifacts of a bygone age.

In the development of human relations one encounters processes similar in effect to those of the earthworm. The surface of the culture conceals many a forgotten deposit; for a time it can suppress aspects of human nature. It can conceal even certain classes of people. Significant human needs or sensitivities are ignored by the dominant trends of the culture. Eventually, however, these hidden needs expose themselves to view, or they may be brought to light by pioneering minds or by men of uneasy conscience.

Anyone who knew Carl Wennerstrom in the period of his doctoral preparations and of his chaplaincy at the hospitals and clinics of the University of Chicago was aware of the fact that he was working in the subsoil. As a religious liberal he was a man of uneasy conscience. He was haunted by the unheeded needs and suffering of troubled people, by the needs of the forgotten man. In his hospital work he encountered every day people of both high and low estate, many of them possessing church affiliation. He wanted to make these people inescapably visible, especially to the churches and the clergy.

Because of his untimely death in 1963, however, Wennerstrom did not bring his doctoral dissertation to completion. But the "material in progress" that appears in the present volume shows that he viewed religious liberalism as a somewhat distorted, lopsided religion because it does not properly recognize and help the forgotten man. Indeed, he was convinced that the typical religious liberal is almost constitutionally insensitive in this respect. In his view, the religious liberal is willing to make dramatic sacrifices for the sake of freedom of conscience or for intellectual integrity or for the improvement of society, but he is not willing to give of himself by entering into affectional communion with the person in distress.

One reason for this pattern is that the liberal is hell-bent toward success. He overlooks his own weaknesses, and he has little patience with the weakness and suffering of others. When he encounters suffering he prefers to form a committee to provide resources for those in need. Moreover, in face of the sufferer he always looks for clear answers to questions and for independent decision and heroically dramatic resolution. In order to maintain this ethos he favors a philanthropic sort of impersonalism for the sake of eliminating error or

achieving a better social order. At the same time he tends
to become bored if he is asked to work out the presuppositions or implications of his outlook. He becomes bored even
by the details involved in effecting social change. He dotes
on being a trailblazer, but wants to maintain distance from
the individual sufferer on whose behalf he enters the fray.

All these aspects of religious liberalism Carl Wennerstrom
brought under the rubrics of rationalism, reformism, dramatics, and distance. It is clear, however, that he did not want
to erase these features of religious liberalism (or of liberal
Protestantism). Rather, he viewed them as ambivalent.
Moreover, he would have admitted that other features are
also to be observed in religious liberalism; but he held that
they are subdominant and not markedly typical.

The dominant features noted in his four paradoxes he
found to be particularly conspicuous among the liberal clergy.
His underlying intention in his project, however, was not to
deliver an indictment. He was committed to the conviction
that liberal Protestantism is the viable heritage of the Reformation for our changing world, and he shared John
Milton's conviction, set forth in *Areopagitica,* that the vin-
dication of this faith demands "even the reforming of reformation itself."

The present volume, with its essays surrounding the rewritten provisional chapters from the Wennerstrom project,
bespeaks the recognition of the striking formulation and
pertinence of the questions he raises. Of special significance
is the fact that these questions are posed in the context
of an importunate concern for pastoral care, a procedure
that is somewhat unique in the current reassessment of the
character and vocation of the liberal dimensions of Protestant Christianity. To the reader it will become readily evident from the essays in this volume that the responsible

11

conduct of pastoral care presupposes, in fact demands, re-flection upon all the dimensions of Christian faith. We editors of course cannot claim that all the dimensions are actually explored herein. Yet the book's contents do indicate major ramifications, theoretical and practical, of pastoral care when it is authentically understood and practiced. To say the least, these essays point to some part of the un-finished business on the agenda of the continuing reform-ing of reformation. They also suggest that this particular mode of reforming began some time ago.

The ways by which this book came into being have been complex and have involved the love and labor of several persons. The guiding force of the whole project, from its inception to its completion, has been the skillful hand of Seward Hiltner. The overall supervision and the editorial work have been his. In the early stages of sorting out the materials of the Wennerstrom project, Coval B. MacDonald was both diligent and imaginative. We hope that an article of his, dealing in detail with Carl Wennerstrom as a person and pastor, may soon find its way into print.

Jeanne Wennerstrom (Mrs. Carl) has done many things for this book. She has typed and retyped, found references, used the duplicating machines, encouraged the editors, and also done the tedious work of making the index. And all this while she was holding a full-time job and taking care of two remarkable children, Ann and Eric Wennerstrom.

Both Charles R. Stinnette and John F. Hayward were colleagues of Carl Wennerstrom. Since they felt toward him both affection and appreciation, it was not difficult to secure their cooperation in the chapters that appear in this volume. Their contributions go far beyond these discussions. Both men helped Jeanne Wennerstrom and the editors on the Carl Wennerstrom materials in addition to writing the chapters in this book. Harry C. Meserve, although not closely associated with Carl Wennerstrom, felt many common sympathies with him and committed himself to the project after reading a few pages of the Wennerstrom material.

As a former member of the Federated Theological Faculty of the University of Chicago, I first became personally acquainted with Carl and Jeanne Wennerstrom when Carl began his theological education at the Divinity School of the University of Chicago. Some years later I had the honor of christening their daughter Ann.

Geographically, we lived very near to each other, but the fact that our conversations often invaded the late hours was due more to propinquity of spirit than of geography. Those conversations brought us inevitably to wrestle with ultimate concerns. This was Carl's nature. In all these discussions about fundamental principles, both Carl and Jeanne Wennerstrom were always deeply involved and committed, open-minded but never detached.

Yet Carl, and Jeanne too, was never willing to neglect the penultimate concerns (this suffering person right here) in favor of the general principles. Carl's death very near the beginning of his promising career constituted a well-nigh irretrievable loss, a loss that only in a small way is partly recovered by this book. Had he lived, he would have made his thesis a kind of incarnation to many people and groups. As it is, what he stood for—and against—must be testified to by this volume.

Of both Jeanne and Carl it may be said that they have probed into the fertile subsoil of the affectional resources human and divine, and that as a consequence they have ever manifested the courage to care.

—JAMES LUTHER ADAMS

13

CARL WENNERSTROM'S LITERARY LEGACY

At the time of his sudden and wholly unexpected death in August, 1963, Carl E. Wennerstrom was "swotting," and making good progress, on the completion of his doctoral dissertation at the University of Chicago, in the field of religion and personality. He passed the comprehensive examinations for this degree in 1956, and had outlined his dissertation project in a prospectus, approved by the appropriate committee, as a prerequisite to taking his examinations. Thus, by 1963, he had been holding this albatross around his doctoral neck for seven years. It is my confident prediction that, had he lived, he would have had a completed draft of his essay within a few months.

Carl Wennerstrom had actually completed at the time of his death two kinds of writings. First, he had written rather more than 150 pages of draft text of his essay, setting forth his basic thesis, discussing and defending it in reference to both experience and available literature, and examining the history of Unitarianism, with special reference to Channing and Parker, for clues

14

in interpreting the present situation. Second, he had tape-recorded interviews with ten Unitarian Universalist ministers, and had had these recordings transcribed, but he had not got round to writing any interpretative comments on them. There are about a hundred thousand words of interview reports, in an original and no copy form.

When Carl Wennerstrom was doing his doctoral residence studies at the University of Chicago, in the years immediately preceding his comprehensive examinations in 1956, I was chairman of the field of religion and personality. In planning his doctoral essay project, Carl Wennerstrom had had my strong encouragement in following his "hunch." His fundamental hunch was that there was a discrepancy between Unitarian theory and Unitarian practice that needed investigation. He himself had had clinical training, had become deeply concerned about pastoral care and pastoral counseling; and he had also, in seminars and other courses, pursued this concern in his doctoral studies. He was quizzical, and even appalled, that no other Unitarian with a primarily theological orientation had preceded him in doctoral studies in this field.

In his clinical and other studies at the University of Chicago, Carl Wennerstrom rubbed shoulders and elbows with both students and faculty who represented a wide range of the Protestant spectrum. Regarding himself, as a Unitarian, as at the left end of this spectrum, at least in some respects, he nevertheless believed that the hunch he had about Unitarians might have a significance far beyond that relatively small group. In the back of his mind was, I believe, a kind of continuum model of United States Protestantism. The fixed point was the left end of the continuum line, firmly occupied by Unitarians and Universalists. But if "liberalism" is what those ministers believe and represent in strong or

15

plus form, then it is also a characteristic which, perhaps in less conspicuous form, may be seen all the way over to the center of the continuum line and perhaps beyond. Thus, Carl Wennerstrom conceived his study of pastoral care in Unitarianism as possibly helping us to understand a discrepancy or a paradox in all degrees of Protestant liberalism.

He was well aware that any critical conception of "liberalism" in theological thought of the nineteenth and twentieth centuries would be vastly more complex and varied than the sense with which he was concerned, i.e., that liberals are people who think a bit like Unitarians only less so! This seems a thoroughly justified position to take, so long as it makes no allegation about exhausting the meaning of "liberalism." After all, Unitarian Universalists do tend to refer to their own ministry as the "liberal ministry," or the "ministry of the liberal churches"; and since the term "liberal" has gone out of general Protestant fashion, few other ministers do call themselves liberals.

It is my own conviction that the content that Carl Wennerstrom assigned as central in Unitarianism, and hence also in liberalism as he intended the term, may be of wider significance than he himself realized. I shall not anticipate the reader's discovery of the four paradoxes set forth by Wennerstrom in the first chapter. But the fact is that not a little of Protestant church life today is more obviously activated by just these characteristics than was true, for example, twenty or thirty years ago. According to the Wennerstrom conception (whatever else liberalism may legitimately mean), the churches generally, and their ministers, are more liberal than they were a short time ago. Since the Wennerstrom analysis is about these characteristics as paradoxes, and since it attempts not only to show permanently positive elements in each characteristic but also to give warning about the negative side as well, it may be that his discussion has a message for much of U.S. Protestant thought and life today that is far broader than the technically limited dimensions of his study itself.

The first two chapters of this volume are my rewritings of the materials that Carl Wennerstrom had himself put into draft dissertation form. I have not hesitated to reorganize and abbreviate, nor have I hesitated to change the style when a point could be made more clearly or sharply. The final style is probably more Hiltner than Wennerstrom. My attentive fidelity has been to Carl Wennerstrom's ideas. All the key ideas are his with one partial exception, the concept of "distance." His manuscript was reaching toward that, but did not quite have the nascent idea pegged conceptually. Since he was so close to it, it seemed to me fair to give him a hand and the idea a name. All the other basic ideas had been fully worked out.

The third chapter gives a summary of the material Carl Wennerstrom had got in his long interviews with ten Unitarian Universalist ministers, done in the one way I felt possible without presuming on the confidentiality of those interviews. The fourth chapter shows Carl Wennerstrom at work in a part of one of the interviews, and this story may be told because the minister concerned has given his consent to publication of the material. In the fifth chapter this anonymous minister gives a spirited and insightful critique of my analysis. Since Wennerstrom had not got round to interpretation of the interview materials, I have simply had to use my best knowledge of the field, of his mind, and of his interests in my presentation of his material.

Among publishers it is a truism that very few doctoral essays are worth publishing in the form of their original preparation. The apparatus and method that need to be exhibited by the dissertation writer to show that he can do specialized research in an area are generally not very exciting to most potential readers; so that even a very good dissertation ordinarily requires much rewriting to become an effective book. Even if Carl Wennerstrom had completed his essay, I suspect his effort would also have needed rewriting for book purposes. As the editor of his actual on-paper legacy, therefore, I have tried to do two things: first, to complete interpretation where he had not been able to do so at the time of his death; and second, to rewrite the material in trans-dissertation terms.

My rewriting of Carl Wennerstrom's actual material does not, however, exhaust his literary legacy. That legacy extends also to the stimulus of his basic ideas to the other contributors to this book. Each of them had access to the rewritten Wennerstrom material, and each of them, in his own way, has been stimulated by it in writing his own contribution.

Whether or not liberals will like what Carl Wennerstrom thought he had found out about them remains to be seen; but of its importance and relevance to them there can be no question. It is my conviction that, although in perhaps a less dramatic or obvious way, precisely the same points are equally relevant and important for a very wide segment of U.S. Protestantism—even for a large number of persons and groups for whom the liberal tag is a bad word. If this particular theological shoe fits, let it not only be worn with a bit of honesty about its ancestry, but also be examined for its strengths as well as for its flaws.

—SEWARD HILTNER

18

LIBERALS AND PASTORAL CARE

Carl E. Wennerstrom

It is my thesis that a curious paradox about pastoral care exists in Unitarian and other liberal Christian churches; that although the paradox has a long history in the liberal movement, it becomes more deplorable every day with the advances now taking place in pastoral care generally, owing both to the resources of the behavioral sciences and to progressive currents of theological thought; and finally, that analysis of the reasons for the paradox, both historical and contemporary, may help liberals to assume their proper and progressive place of leadership in the pastoral care movement.

The basic nature of the paradox is this. When the insights of Freud, and then of many others from various fields of medicine, psychology, and other social sciences, began to illuminate the complex nature of man's inner life, his personal development, and his social relationships, Unitarians and other liberals had, in principle, the least quarrel of any religious groups with the startling findings of these sciences. If they had not quite worshiped science, they had nevertheless been

19

thoroughly committed to it and to any truth it could discover. They should, therefore, have been the most receptive and open-minded of all about new scientific findings, including the implications of the findings for the work of the ministers and churches. Innocent of any sharp dividing line between sacred and secular, they were committed to see the implications of scientific findings for every realm and dimension of life including religion and the church.

But the fact is, they did not pursue, across the board, the implications of the new data. On a selective basis they did pay attention to it. A good illustration of the selective attention (and inattention) may be shown, on the one hand, by the considerable proportion of liberal ministers who from the start became advocates of the modern mental health movement; but most of whom, at the same time, neither rethought their understanding of man on the basis of the same scientific data being used by the mental health movement, nor made any appreciable alterations in their work of pastoral care with their people.

In calling this situation "paradox," I am perhaps being too gentle. In some respects it is a real and not just an apparent contradiction. If there is advocacy of science, but attentiveness only to such aspects of its findings and implications as contain no subtle threat to one's own convictions, that would be actual contradiction; and there is evidence of some of this. But in the main, the situation is more subtle than that. Not many, even among the most optimistic or rationalistic, will fail to admit under pressure that man has been shown by Freud and others to have more complex potentialities for evil than had been envisioned by most of our liberal forebears. Yet, even with such an admission there may be little or no follow-through in terms either of a systematic rethinking of a doctrine of man, or of the need for pastoral care. So, all things considered, paradox seems closer to the actual situation than contradiction.

Progress Right and Center

I became interested in pastoral care while a theological student at the Divinity School of The University of Chicago. In both theoretical and supervised clinical courses, guided by people including Seward Hiltner and Carl R. Rogers, I studied side by side with Congregational, Presbyterian, Baptist, Lutheran, Methodist, and many other kinds of students across nearly the whole spectrum of Protestant conviction. It was, above all, the supervised clinical study that compelled me to rethink my assumed liberal position about pastoral care. In ministry, under guidance, to persons confronting deep suffering and pain, and often the prospect of early death, I was forced, even in student days, to a new order of reflection. But the theoretical work that went along with the clinical was important too. We examined the history of pastoral care, and I became more and more astonished to find Unitarian and other liberal literature almost blank on the subject.

Were we really as bad as that? Or were we liberals so very good and noble that we never needed understanding, consolation, or comfort in pain or suffering, never made mistakes about our marriages, always looked death straight in the eye, never drank too much, were always kind and tender and loving to our families and employees and bosses, never got neuroses or depressions or paranoid delusions, always found childbirth and hysterectomies and menopauses a cinch, were always unruffled before mental deficiency or physical handicaps, and never beat our breasts vainly about the economic or class arrangements of society? To be sure,

21

not even our worst enemy could accuse us of being without a *social* conscience on most of these things. We have always been concerned—*for other people.* But, like Shylock, hath not a liberal also these things, at times? Do we really believe ourselves so good and brave and noble that we may never need such help ourselves? Do we secretly regard our principles as a kind of insurance policy against life's slings and arrows, so that we say to ourselves surreptitiously, "There but for the grace of being a liberal might go I"?

Why, I kept asking on the one hand, especially in view of the open and generous spirit toward scientific inquiry that has characterized the liberal churches, have they had such poor representation in the modern movement to bang the head of theology against the personality studies and vice versa? And why, against expectation, has this movement contained so many persons from the center and right-wing churches of Protestantism? Even if the right-wingers were slow, contrasted with liberals, to get into such questions as those posed by Freud, why have they, after they began to do so, pursued their investigations with such vigor and persistence?

Virtually all serious students of the processes of direct psychological help—whether counseling, psychotherapy, or guidance—have shown that the helper must begin with the person where he really is, problems, concerns, conflicts, negativities, aspirations, delusions, and all. At first glance, one would expect the more orthodox clergyman to find it genuinely difficult to focus in this way upon the actually existing condition and situation of the person. For would not he, whatever his particular version of commitment to the saving power of Christ, be so eager to testify to that as the root source of help for his parishioner that he would feel disloyal if he really "accepted" the parishioner as he now is, conflicts,

negativities, and all? And no doubt there are relatively orthodox clergy of whom this is still true. But among serious
students of pastoral care, we find something else. Indeed,
we often find that it is the very motive power of the understanding of Christian commitment that enables the clergyman truly to accept his parishioner where he is.

An illustration of this motive power may be seen in some
Trinitarian ministers I have known and in the meaning to
them of the doctrine of the Holy Spirit. Whether or not such
ministers are correct to their tradition in understanding the
Holy Spirit as they do, they feel that the presence of God's
Holy and Comforting Spirit beside a bed of pain, for
instance, enables them to relax and thus be more available
to the person in his actual pain. Even the mystery of the
pain itself can be faced as such, without the compulsion to
explain it when no explanation can possibly be valid. Some
such conviction is certainly basic to being genuinely available
to the actual situation. Traditional Protestant theology, to
be sure, has had a great and bewildering variety of views
about the Holy Spirit—all the way from so identifying it
with the church as virtually to cut off any novelty on God's
part, over to the ecstatic phenomena of glossolalia, or alleged
instantaneous healings, or other "second blessings" of many
kinds. But if a soberly serious pastor can believe that God
himself, through the Holy Spirit, reduces his anxiety and
fret to "get results," increases his capacity for calm but
involved attentiveness to the person as he actually is, lets
him be more empathic to concrete suffering with no risk of
losing his own identity, then such a pastor has a resource
that has been denied, literally or in terms of equivalents,
to the Unitarian.

For reasons that are not relevant here, and which may
still be sound, Unitarians and some other liberals have

found unpalatable the Trinitarian doctrine including, in this instance, the notion of God as Holy Spirit. From a strictly psychological point of view, what does this mean when the Unitarian minister is beside the bed of pain and his appropriate human sympathies are caught up in a strong desire to help or ease or alleviate the pain? Under this stress he is altogether likely to turn inside himself for an answer, as if he were to say to himself, "I've got to find something that will help this person." He may then turn to something external, some rational explanation of the crisis, a theory of development, or something else. The content of this external is unlikely to be like orthodox Protestantism; but I am impressed by how often the form is the same. And yet whether the content is true, false, or dubious, it diverts the minister from full attentiveness to the situation of the person before him, who is suffering. He is trying to be "answer man" to the person's pain. But the one answer he can really give is his presence and his undivided concern. The pain is still, in part, mystery. Can a minister in such a situation do without some equivalent (at least psychologically) of the doctrine of the Holy Spirit? If he has no such equivalent, he will, however unwittingly, deny the mystery altogether and believe he is making himself fully available; while in actual fact it may well be he, and not his parishioner, who is evading that aspect of the total situation that is essential to the sole kind of release or freedom now possible. To use a bit of psychoanalytic jargon, are the liberal minister's goals in such a situation so over-determined that he is unable to give himself fully and truly to the person in the actuality of his predicament? If, for good and sufficient theological reasons, some of us liberals can not have God as Holy Spirit beside us, what can we have instead that will prevent us from the impossible answer of trying to be answer man to everything?

Reasons for the Liberal Paradox

It will be my argument that there is a chain of interrelated factors producing the liberal paradox about pastoral care, and thus that no single factor can be pounced on with a "this-is-it" attitude of confident diagnosis. But because I shall cite several factors and allege them to be influential, it should not be concluded that the several factors are adventitious, products of happenstance, or entities in themselves. They are, in my judgment, dynamically interrelated. Thus, they tend to reinforce one another. Anyone like myself, therefore, who wants to alter the pastoral care *status quo* must somehow bring a fresh perspective to the whole set of interconnected factors, or else his argument will produce no change.

My discussion of the factors producing the liberal paradox about pastoral care will proceed, generally speaking, from the more obvious to the more significant. Actually, the more obvious factors *are* less significant. Let the defending reader reserve his big guns for the factors to be discussed later.

Rationalism. Faith, from the beginning of the Unitarian movement, was quite genuinely in God; but it was also a kind of faith in man, and in man's potentialities, intended to be corrective of the denigratory view of man—a "worm" and "totally depraved"—as set forth in most Protestant theologies of the time. The connection between man and God was never lost. When the early liberals alleged some justified confidence in man's mind and intellect, in his capacity to reason and plan, in his ability to inquire and study and

25

know, they felt that these were the handiwork of God, who made them all possible. They could be committed to science as inquiry because they believed that the truth discovered would be God's truth, and hence, finally, truth for man, truth in man's interest. Revelation was felt to be a continuing process; new light would continue to come forth. Through his inquiries, man could confidently seek that light, knowing that it was God who had created it.

There is in this position, I would allege today, nobility and a great deal of truth; and there is also genuine religious faith. *With* the faith, a person can examine possible contradictions when new discoveries are made; and still, in his faith, remain courageous about human potentialities. But of course since the general cast of thought is along rational lines, he may also, however unwittingly, become rationalistic; i.e., select from emerging findings those that support or do not threaten his thought-structure and either ignore the others or allege that the others, now understood, may be changed. Rationalism has become a pejorative term. Whether or not liberals are in fact rationalistic in such a sense, must depend not on their having ultimate faith in some kind of potential for reason and intelligence (for without that we could have no "universe") but in their exercising of reason and intelligence at whatever level, and in whatever time schedule, that may legitimately be counted on. The movement cannot, I think, be held guiltless of sometimes trying to oversimplify the complex, or of anticipating too much too soon, "if only people would be reasonable."

When the findings of Freud, and then of others, appeared, there was a threat, not necessarily to the ultimate power of some kind of educated reason, in which Freud also believed, but to any kind of foreshortened view of man's interior and relational complexities, and to the possible time schedule

26

for getting ahead with his human problems. Freud's iceberg metaphor (eight-ninths of man's mind was alleged to be inaccessible by ordinary means) was not the kind of declaration liberals most hoped to hear.

Not long ago an older liberal minister, a man of great achievements and deserved distinction, told me of his first encounter with the findings of Freud. His honest word was "shock." As never before, he said, he was appalled, upon confronting Freud's idea of the unconscious, with the strength of the evil he found there, even though it was locked in battle with the urge toward the good. His own attention, he said, had been upon the potentialities of the human being: the promise of his intellect, the strength of his reasonableness, the potential purity, and with more being discovered all the time. For a moment, he said, Freud had nearly shaken his faith from its roots. But then he said: "Nevertheless, I believe in Man. It is he alone who has the power to overcome the evils within him through the great gifts of reason and intellect. He need not succumb to the dark forces at work in these nether regions of the psyche. He can indeed yet be master of his soul." Here is wisdom, insight, and, above all, courage. And yet I think there is also a clinging to naïve rationalism.

Rationalism is, I think, a factor in the liberal paradox about pastoral care. But it is a mixed factor. A true faith in reason can, even after shock, begin to come to terms with new complexities or new evils that may be revealed; it can approach them courageously, sometimes because its belief in reason transcends the shock. There is no solution in "irrationalism." But at the same time, the shock may bring a temptation toward partial denial, toward inattention to anything that can not be wiped away by rational social action. My appraisal of liberal rationalism is, therefore, ambivalent.

Some trends in it went one way positively, toward courageous confrontation; and another part slunk into inattentive
and negative denial.

Reformism. Dorothea Dix, Henry Bellows, Gridley Howe,
and Florence Nightingale are excellent illustrations of constructive liberal "reformism." Long before the modern mental health movement, for instance, Dorothea Dix was ex-
posing the often shameful and inhumane conditions in mental hospitals, and was going right to headquarters, i.e., the
state legislatures, to call for fundamental improvement.
With real passion, strong argument, and great energy, she
went across the nation on this unique errand of mercy and
reform. And she got at least some results. Indeed, current
new interest in studying her work may eventually demonstrate even more actual influence than her biographers so
far have claimed.

And yet Dorothea Dix's principles, on which she staked
her reformist policies, we now know to have been partly
mistaken. She utilized the faulty mental hospital statistics,
as Albert Deutsch showed, that were available in her time.[1]
Thus, unwittingly, she promised more than was actually
possible. The statistics she had favored contained a kind
of optimism about how many could be released if they had
humane care. Today we know that the direction of her
thought and conviction was perfectly correct. But by un-
intentionally promising too much too soon, she invited some
disillusionment, and some of it actually came.

Despite their small numbers, liberals were prominent in
the pioneering social welfare efforts. They were sensitive
to slums, and poverty, and prejudice, and many other social

[1] Albert Deutsch, *The Mentally Ill in America* (New York: Columbia University Press, 1946).

ills. As already noted, they were among the first to support the modern mental health movement. The work of the Unitarian Service Committee, for instance, speaks for itself. Sociological findings were taken into account very early. Reform efforts have always contained realism. And yet one sometimes wonders if an unduly optimistic base, like Dorothea Dix's, must always be used in relation to such efforts. To use an old analogy, have not many of these efforts been too optimistic about how quickly an effective fence could be built at the head of the cliff, so that no ambulance would be needed to pick up victims at its bottom?

As with rationalism, I believe reformism is ambiguous concerning the liberal paradox of pastoral care. The general intelligence of liberal efforts (cf. Dorothea Dix) has saved reformism, at all times, from futility and has brought demonstrable social gains in many areas. At the same time, it may very well have minimized the continuing need for ambulances, as it overestimated the speed and certainty with which reform could prevent and alleviate various ills.

Dramatics. There is in the liberal movement, and especially in its ministers, a kind of cryptic, self-dramatic sense, which is perhaps the liberal's way of trying to deal with, at the same time, the question of power and that of professional self-identity. The liberal is a liberal partly because he is for the right social causes. But if he is really for them, then he will be involved in some kind of leadership of them. Thus, he is never more a liberal than when at some general community meeting he is making the most compelling and convincing speech in favor of such a cause. I suspect he feels more liberal there than he does when preaching to his own people in his own church. That outreach, above all, is what a liberal minister should be doing.

29

This is not, in the pejorative sense of the term, publicity seeking; for that term implies a kind of chameleon-like accommodation which is absent from the liberal. Nor is it applause seeking, in that the major satisfactions derived are from the approval of others. The true liberal could, I think, be equally content with a large audience or a very small one, provided he felt that an impact was being made through him on the basis of the sheer force of facts, moral convictions, and sound and even passionate reasoning. In such situations the liberal is an actor, happily playing the role which reveals and releases, and does not mask or conceal, his true sense of his identity. The occasion permits him to be most himself. If everyone present already had all the facts, already agreed on the basic principles, already were united that something should be done, and if all that were left were the tedious and detailed examination of how to go about it, my guess is that the liberal would tend to be a bit bored. But give him a bit of opposition, of ignorance, of faintheartedness, or of futility, and he is at his dramatic best.

As a hospital chaplain, I have often thought that liberals are biased in favor of surgery against, for example, internal medicine. For surgery is decisive. You live or die, cut it out or fail to do so, improve the condition radically or discover that it can not be improved at all. It is not like "trying" this or that, such a frequent and necessary feature of internal medicine. Liberals, at least metaphorically, make good surgeons, but have less aptitude as internists.

Part of this self-dramatic sense of the liberal may be descendant from the theological "covered wagon" of the early liberal frontier. The early liberal felt himself on a kind of theological prairie or desert. The alleged oases at which Calvinists, Lutherans, Baptists, and Anglicans found their food and water were mirages or illusions, according to him.

He had to cut loose from them, and start digging for water or cultivating his own food. Sometimes the early liberal developed an exaggerated sense of independence. Only what *he* dug up or discovered was real to him. Hence, his sense of identity was most at ease when he was digging or dredging or cultivating, so to speak, on his own. He would have felt thwarted had a food and water wagon come by to take care of his needs. This sense of what might be called "dedicated dramatic digging" has gone on. Liberal dramatics is not playacting; it is very real indeed. It may be equally frustrated if the digging proves fruitless, or it is discovered to be unnecessary. Not the play but the dramatic process is the thing; for here, above all, one finds his true vocation.

If the liberal found the basis for meaning in existing texts, doctrines, and the like, even though he should bring novelty of perspective to them, he would be tempted to regard his own digging as unnecessary. He may, then, like the desert explorer, tend to search for meanings in the episodic and circumstantial realms of life. What he digs up may not be without importance; but he may be less than honest in admitting that it is his dramatic digging-up of it, rather than its explored implications, that make it exciting for him. It is not just that he dislikes routine or repetition. He wants to blaze trails all the time.

I have sometimes wondered, incidentally, if this dramatic penchant for trailblazing, and this boredom with any partially established trail, may not put the liberal *en rapport* with the hero myths of so many cultures, in which the hero always, despite his trials and tribulations, finally slays the dragon and gets the girl; as against, for example, the New Testament parable of the prodigal son, where the son's trailblazing effort was a fiasco and his self-identity was restored only by his father's forgiveness. Is some part of liberal dramatics an unwitting attempt to compensate for unacknowledged interior weakness? My guess is that the dramatics, as I have called the tendency, is a bit of this, as well as being obviously, very often, in the social interest. So far as our liberal paradox of pastoral care is concerned, therefore, dramatics may also be ambiguous.

Distance. In trying to get at a very subtle but very important characteristic of liberals, I have borrowed from sociology the concept of "social distance." According to this notion both individuals and groups develop patterns of relationship involving optimal (i.e., not too close nor too far away) social distance and social intimacy. If you call the English clubman "John" instead of "Webley-Jones," even after lunching with him for fifteen years, you may violate optimal distance in upper-class English culture. If, you call Johnny Bud Jones, "Mr. Jones," after two days of association in the American South, instead of "Johnny" or "Johnny Bud," you will also violate it. That is, there is no absolute, transcultural standard of optimal social distance. But within any culture or subculture the normative conception of optimal social distance is of the greatest importance.

As a kind of subculture, Unitarianism in particular and the liberal churches in general reveal quite particular assumptions about the optimal social distance. If the prototypical or paradigmatic liberal could have things just as he wished, I believe that his optimal way of helping people would be as follows. A certain kind of need on the part of a number of people would be revealed (e.g., affliction with mental illness, lack of job skills, discrimination due to race or color, difficulty in securing education, etc.). The liberal would then get facts from the experts on the particular problem, join in community leadership to mobilize resources; and programs would evolve that included the appropriate resources, both experts and community representatives. The minute any person who had this kind of problem came to the liberal's attention, he could be referred sympathetically to the new resources. Imaginatively and empathetically the liberal could think of the process of the person's being helped by the direct helping persons, feeling a real share in having provided the resources out of which the help comes. The psychology of this must be, in part, like that of the laboratory man who discovers or adapts a drug that proves to be specific for this or that kind of ill. He himself never administers an actual dose to any single person. But he takes a legitimate satisfaction in having prepared, or helped to prepare, the resource that helps many persons. Thus, a great deal of liberal social action is related to the direct helping of persons as laboratory ingenuity is related to the direct healing of personal ills. For the liberal the development and evocation of appropriate social resources is a kind of Holy Grail. It makes help definite, assured, and permanent within the limitations of the problem's severity. It also renders unnecessary any intimate contact between the individual liberal and the individual person in need.

The more authoritative and certain the resources of help on this or that kind of problem, the greater the chances of the person's getting the help he needs. This is the positive, humanitarian, and people-concerned aspect of "liberal distance." But it is equally true that the more certain the resource, the less likely the possibility that the liberal will have to sweat it out in the valley of uncertainty with the person in need. The implicit fear of intimacy seems not a fear of closeness as such, as in friendship, where Unitarians may be as warm as Southern Baptists, but rather a fear of "suffering intimacy." Or perhaps "intimacy with uncertainty" is a better term. From a psychological perspective the issue is: What could arouse the liberal's feelings of anxiety, or dread, or jittery insecurity? And the answer seems to be, not personal intimacy as such, but intimacy with someone whose problem is such that: (1) there is no certain solution whatever course is followed; (2) there is manifest suffering now, and there will be in the future; (3) there is a relationship with the person that is at least as much sharing the feeling-dimensions of the unsolved problem as it is moving toward a solution. In such a situation the Idea, the Program, and the Course of Action, whatever their content, are insufficient to effect a solution. In the face of such situations our standard liberal wants to be somewhere else, preferably out in the social laboratories where research and social concern and programming are finding out how just this kind of problem may eventually be solved. But where he does not want to be is with the person who has this problem, and has it now.

I am tempted to say that the liberal wants to have a kind of prophet's relationship to people in need. But prophet can be interpreted in more ways than one. If the central notion about the true prophet is that he endeavors deeply to "speak on God's behalf," or to speak on behalf of the very deepest values inherent in the situation, then I believe the liberal does want, even consciously sometimes, to come at any situation or problem with a prophetic stance. But as the history of prophets and prophecy shows, all the way from the biblical "sons of the prophets" to our own day, even the truest prophet is always tempted to define his prophecy, at least implicitly, in other than the normative sense of speaking on God's behalf.

He is tempted to think his prophetic function renders unnecessary any genuine involvement with the present mess

34

because he heralds the new age and the new potentialities. Because he is genuinely concerned with human values, he is tempted to skip quickly over any specific sympathies for particular persons in particular situations. He may even be tempted, in the worst misdefinition of prophecy of all, to regard prophecy as prediction, and prediction as dependent on capacity to influence, and capacity to influence as persuasive eloquence, and persuasive eloquence as, above all else, talking. Thus, in a cryptic and unacknowledged way, he may believe that speaking on God's behalf is proclamation rather than "bringing a message." Psychologically he may be more Barthian than he realizes. Let me be thy prophet, O Lord, but spare me from having to be a Western Union boy taking particular messages to particular people at particular addresses, most especially if they want me to hang around and listen to them.

I am also tempted to say the liberal is impatient; but impatience, like prophecy, may mean more than one thing. Rightly and ethically the liberal believes himself to be impatient in the sense that he does not yield passively to any particular *status quo* that involves unfulfillment or suffering. May he, however, be impatient as well in other ways that are more ambiguous? For example, may he be impatient —even bored—with any specific person or instance of a problem or suffering because, seeing this instance always in the light of the more general problem, he wants to get on with solving this *kind* of problem and not be deflected by this person's particular problem? May his impatience be more repressive and compensatory than he realizes, not serving mainly the function of trying to solve this (clearly defined) kind of problem, but serving actually the function of concealing the existence of problems that cannot be clearly defined? In the social and behavioral sciences today there are not a few persons whose decisions about what they will investigate are made less in terms of the importance of the problem than in terms of the definiteness of the available methods of study. May some liberal impatience be like that?

I am tempted to say, finally, that the liberal's notions of optimal distance imply that he must be a leader at all times and places. Positively, being a leader in his sense means having social sensitivity and social responsibility and, if need be, social courage. It also means having constant commerce, through persuasion not coercion, with the community beyond the religious fellowship. Neither in the community nor in the church can one become just another member and rest content with it.

As modern studies of democratic leadership have shown, however, the real leader (who of course must disdain equally authoritarian domination and anarchic irresponsibility) can evoke the initiative and responsibility of others only by risking and involving his own. Detachment is not enough. The better the leader, the more encouraged others are to assume responsible leadership. In terms of involvement, the leader becomes more like other members, not so much because *he* has changed as because he has helped *them* to change in a responsible direction. But his leadership is not defined, at the start or the finish, by his lack of involvement. Social distance declines as others assume more responsibility. No good leadership process finds social distance the same at the beginning and the end. Consequently, it is not proper to define leadership relationships in terms of any particular order of social distance, good for all time. Against this kind of analysis, does the liberal, while no doubt condemning all forms of "authoritarian leadership," nevertheless insist on defining leadership itself precisely as authoritarians do, i.e., as a relationship that never changes with time and inter-action? Does he tend, however cryptically or backhandedly, to conceive leadership as a fixed status rather than as a changing function?

Our standard liberal, I believe, feels most at home when there is a safe distance between him and the actual sufferings of particular people. He is unlike the thoughtless or uncon-cerned, in that some part of him does suffer with sufferers. The last thing he would do is to let the rest of the world go by. In a not insignificant sense, he assumes some responsi-bility for the sufferings of the world. Perhaps he would be shocked to be told that his desire to alleviate the sufferings of others implies a belief in some kind of vicarious atonement with himself as one of the vicars, but this seems to be true. He may not regard his concern and empathy for the suf-ferings of others to be "taking up the cross," but in actual fact he believes that what hurts one hurts all.

Yet with all these admirable characteristics, the liberal still does not want to get too close. Metaphorically speaking, the first liberal (so far as the distance notion goes, at any rate) might well have been the man who helped Jesus carry the cross to the place where he was crucified. With a job to be done, he was there. With energy to be spent, he had it. And, in carrying a heavy cross, he was not drawn too close together with Jesus. Once the spot had been reached and the outcome was certain he dropped from sight; we hear no more of this early liberal in the New Testament. Perhaps he was off to the Circuit Court, hoping against hope to get a reversal of the conviction, and having the courage to try. Or he may have been investigating the future support of Jesus' family, or the burial arrangements, or he may even have been getting up a petition to Rome about Pilate. What he was about was no doubt of great potential significance. But at the place of crucifixion, he was absent once the cross had been delivered. For a liberal, the optimal social distance.

Conclusion. This analysis is certainly not exhaustive of the reasons that may lie behind what has been called the "liberal paradox" about pastoral care, but I hope it has both illuminated some aspects of what has produced the present situation and provoked further reflections that may lead to a still more penetrating appraisal by others.

In making a stab at this kind of analysis, I believe I am exemplifying true liberal principles. No category with which I have dealt has been treated as simply negative. Good words need to be said for rationalism, reformism, dramatics, and distance. Rightly understood, I believe in them all. Any church or religious faith that keeps them in the subbasement is likely to become rigid, attached to the *status quo,* insensitive to contemporary forms of suffering, cowardly before the extent of the need, or romantic about saving people one by one through such pietistic devices as family nights, handshakes, and altar calls.

But if my analysis holds, the fact is that the excellence and truth of each point have been sadly tarnished in the execution. Even in what is very best about us, we liberals too have sinned and fallen short; or more aptly, perhaps, have fallen out of the wrong side of the bed. Our rationalism has been used not just to defend reason and science and learning and inquiry, but also to defend us from feeling and involvement and emotion and concreteness. Our reformism has led us not only to construction after criticism of the *status quo,* but also to such a predilection for blazing trails that we are equally startled to find wholly unmet needs or needs met by the "wrong people." Our dramatics help us to stand up and be counted, and on the right issues too, but they also make us poor at following through. Our sense of optimal distance happily prevents us from equating acquiescence or resignation with justice or fulfillment. It sends us on ahead to prepare the way, to prevent, to educate, to get at root causes, to mobilize public opinion, to serve, if need be, as the community's conscience. Yet our unacknowledged anxiety too often keeps us away from the places where concrete suffering is being faced or endured or encountered.

The Care of Souls: Motivation and Knowledge

As John T. McNeill's *History of the Cure of Souls* makes clear, there has never been a group in Christian history that did not devote some kind of serious attention to the care of souls, i.e., to persons and whatever needs viewed either individually or collectively were felt to be theirs.[2] Even though not a little in the history of soul care took the form of disciplining individual offenders against group mores, even there the intent was restoration of the person to the community and to right relationship with God. And although the other kind of soul care—comforting the bereaved, encouraging the sick and afflicted, giving moral support in the face of both depression and oppression— did not get written up so often as did the deeds of offenders, it was never absent in any Christian group.

The traditional motivation for soul care, therefore, while not innocent of a defensive stance in protecting the religious community, has always finally rooted itself in concern for the ultimate welfare of the person. Forms and definitions have varied widely. But common to all has been the motif of helping, or healing, or shepherding (pastoring).

[2] (New York: Harper & Brothers, 1951).

The modern movement to reexamine and reemphasize pastoral care began in the nineteen-twenties. The motivations behind this movement, when compared and contrasted with previous Christian periods, have not been strikingly different at root. But one fact about this movement has set it apart from all previous periods of pastoral care, namely, the way it has sought knowledge about how to help. A corollary has been that increased knowledge of how to help has tended to deepen the commitment to the helping processes.

Suppose a minister to be making a pastoral call in older days. The chances are that he would quickly whip out a Bible or a prayer. He might or might not be intuitively shrewd about the underlying needs of the person or family. But he would certainly not have our modern knowledge of psychodynamics that would enable him, during the conversation itself, to move step by step toward a better understanding of that need. Furthermore, his readiness to provide the treatment before he had made a competent diagnosis strikes us today as on the authoritarian side.

As liberalizing trends advanced in most of the churches, it became less routine to whip out the Bible at the start of the pastoral call. Whatever might be done during the latter part of the call, it was increasingly recognized that a more personal relationship had to be established. In some sense, the minister had to listen too. This period brought about the "duty" conception of pastoral calling. The minister took the punishment of wearing out both his shoe leather and his ears in calling upon and engaging in conversation with his parishioners, so that he could get to know them and hence preach to them (in church) more effectively. In this period nobody thought pastoral care was *inherently* interesting. It often degenerated into mere social chitchat; or, in reaction against that, went back to Bible thumping.

If the older, authoritarian period was like treatment without diagnosis, the era that followed had neither diagnosis nor treatment. Historically speaking, its one merit was in preparing the way for a new kind of relationship between diagnosis and treatment, to continue the metaphor. And the cornerstone of the modern pastoral care movement has been its understanding, its still rudimentary but growing knowledge, about how to understand particular persons with particular needs, i.e., a kind of diagnosis.

It is not necessary here to review the content of this new knowledge, for some of which the minister is indebted to explorers and practitioners in other professions like medicine and psychiatry, social work, and clinical psychology, among many. But the general character of this knowledge is worth noting. It does have, on the one hand, general or comprehensive principles, i.e., knowledge of "man," so to speak. But it has, on the other hand, a clinical or concrete orientation, so that principles are used to illuminate the individual instance, and experience with the specific situation is used in turn to shed light on the general principles. The two foci of knowledge, in other words, are seen to be related, to be mutually necessary; so that the minister cannot be professionally responsible if he has one without the other.

When knowledge is seen in this way, then it tends to reinforce the motivation for pastoral care. If the activities of pastoral helping are not seen as leading toward knowledge, then we have the duty conception of pastoral care. If those activities are regarded only as applying knowledge learned elsewhere, then we are likely to have the older authoritarian version of pastoral care. But when an intimate and mutual relationship is seen between learning through concrete situations and reflection on general principles, then motivation

41

may be released both from the boredom of duty and the retreat to attempted control.

Where do liberals stand in this more general picture? Certainly they never had the extremes, either of authoritarianism or boredom, that characterized some other Christian groups. But they were not in the earlier period wholly innocent of authoritarianism in actual practice (treatment before concrete diagnosis) even if the authority on which their action rested was less external and objectivized. Similarly, they were not devoid in the subsequent period of duty and boredom about actual attempts to help, especially when the persons involved were not capable of "talking ideas." Motivation was strong, however, in any dealings with persons who could talk ideas. But if they could talk ideas, the presumption was that they were open to "education" and did not need help.

"Ideas," in the sense intended here, may have two kinds of meanings. On the one hand, they may mean exactly what the liberal hopes they mean, freedom from special personal needs and capacity to invest intelligently in the world beyond and its needs. Where that is in fact true, then pastoral care properly gives way to education, social action, and programming. But ideas, on the other hand, may also mean rationalization in the Freudian sense, defensive smokescreens over essentially personal problems. When this is the situation, very great skill is needed in pastoral care; for one is equally wrong to take ideas literally at face value or to try to expose them with clever blasts. Ideas, and a person's capacity to communicate with and through them, are then ambiguous. To be predisposed to ideas, in the sense suggested, is to invite ambiguity. And since ideas quite often are, in the same person, partly a reflection of his freedom and partly a concealment of the limitations on his freedom, the tendency to see ideas as unambiguously positive in themselves invites a distorted understanding of the "whole person." It is of this that I believe liberals tend to be guilty.

Most liberals have read some Freud. The general-principles side of their knowledge is likely to be reasonably good. But they have seldom learned to deal with the principles in relation to specific persons and situations, and to use the involvement in concrete situations to illuminate the general principles. Thus, unlike many other ministers today, their knowledge tends not to reinforce their motivation toward pastoral care.

We come now to a final point about the relationship of knowledge to motivation in pastoral care, the understanding of human weakness and human strength. Concerning obvious human weakness—the widows and orphans of the Bible —the liberal is traditional in his judgments and usually strongly motivated in his social action to give help and protection. The liberal is less happy, however, about nonobvious weakness; and he is disconcerted perhaps most of all to find underlying strength in apparent weakness.

From the point of view of modern psychiatry and related disciplines, the person who can openly acknowledge an interior weakness (as, for instance, by seeking help in relation to it) is regarded as thereby demonstrating great potential strength. The capacity to *feel* anxiety is strength, as against the development of various orders of symptoms to prevent one from the pain of feeling the anxiety. All underlying and nonobvious psychic strength, therefore, emerges in relationships like pastoral care as ambiguity. If the pastor can not tolerate ambiguity, he is automatically distorting and underestimating the potential strengths in the person with whom he is dealing. And if that is so, then it is a fair inference that *his* anxiety threshold is low, i.e., that

43

his tendency to play down the actual ambiguity in the situation is itself a kind of symptom.

Perhaps we can now say that the most basic aspect of the paradox of the liberal minister's attitude to pastoral care is that he, more than other ministers, tends to be panicked by the paradoxical and ambiguous character of human intra-psychic problems. He will go to any lengths to get resources for persons whose problems and needs are unambiguous, e.g., widows and orphans. And he will converse—responsibly too—for hours with any one strong enough to have ideas. But mix the two up in any combination of ambiguity, and the liberal wants to be somewhere else.

Is it going too far to suggest that the Unitarian or other liberal is more activated than he realizes by "the quest for certainty"? Boldly and, I am convinced, very often rightly, he has set aside various traditional forms alleged to guarantee certainty and security. This setting aside he shares with the existentialist; but he is, I believe, less narcissistic and self-preoccupied, and also less generally rebellious, than the existentialist. His belief *in* man's potentialities is genuine and not defiant against the universe. Thus, Unitarianism has a much more religious kind of attitude than does Stoicism or existentialism.

But even though the liberal has renounced many of the traditional props of religious certainty, has he really transformed the interior need for certainty, or the feeling of threat in the face of uncertainty? Against what I wish were true, I have become reluctantly convinced that most liberals seem to have used up their "capacity for uncertainty" in what they have renounced, and expect as their reward to be given clear-cut situations from then on. Larger social situations, e.g., progress in race relations, can be handled effectively; for, whatever the long-term ambiguities about them, there can be little doubt about the proper immediate direction. But when the liberal confronts the individual person, or family, in any kind of depth dimension, then the security base is most threatened. In the most confusing of all human paradoxes, weakness may prove to be strength, and strength, weakness. Values have to be revalued. The criteria of strength and weakness, certainty and security, must be reappraised. Before this, the liberal is tempted to quail.

Liberals were right, I believe, to set aside many of the traditional supports within the Christian tradition. But this level of emancipation is not enough. The compulsive quest for certainty may reside not only in the allegation of indifensible objectivities, but also in a distaste for the dimensions of ambiguity in human psychic reality. The liberal emancipation should extend to this distaste. If we can make it do so, we can give existentialism a run for its money, as we once did with supernaturalism. The strength of existentialism, psychologically speaking, is its acceptance of the real ambiguity in human psychic life. Its weakness is that it confuses the confrontation of ambiguity with the act of faith. Liberals have real faith; but this can reach modern man only if it does not, in its assertion, denigrate the actual ambiguity of the human situation.

A true liberal advance in pastoral care could help a lot of intelligent people who are not now being helped when they need it, could give existentialism a run for its money, and just might assist some theologizing about pastoral care in the main-line Protestant groups to avoid atavistic retreats to primitivity. The stakes are large. They extend beyond the liberal constituency. It is high time that liberals get a real theory of pastoral care, and go to work practicing it— even on liberals.

45

CHANNING, PARKER, AND PEOPLE

Carl E. Wennerstrom

William Ellery Channing and Theodore Parker were, by any criteria that may be applied, among the greatest leaders of early Unitarianism. If the purpose of the present discussion were a comprehensive history of Unitarianism, of course other names would have to be included. But for our purposes—examining the factors in early Unitarianism and liberalism that serve as background for the present situation in pastoral care as already described—Channing and Parker provide the ideal avenue.

Channing and Parker had much in common. Both were true liberals. Both put high value on the mind and on reason, and both were committed to the use of both rational and emotional dimensions of man to help him move toward virtue and true morality. Both rejected the prevailing supernaturalism; and both, while deeply devoted to God and to the Bible as providing, if properly interpreted, reliable revelation about God's nature and intent, rejected God as a dictator, and instead saw man as something like God's

46

partner in the business of moving toward knowledge and virtue. Both, furthermore, in actual practice saw their main task in their public ministries. Even though both advocated also the importance of the private and pastoral dimensions of ministry, both found their actual normative definitions of ministry from the other realm. Both were influenced by transcendentalism, but both became critical of the abstractional realms to which extremities of that movement led. Both had a strong streak of piety that appeared mainly in a moral form, although both "pietism" and "moralism" are inappropriate words to describe their religiously oriented moral convictions. And the present list of commonalities is far from exhaustive.

Yet Channing and Parker were also poles apart, above all in personality characteristics. Channing said of himself, "I am strong before the multitude, but weak before the individual." He was always occupied with "great soaring thoughts." No matter where he was, a "subject" was always occupying his attention. A biographer wrote that Channing found it difficult to respond "quickly to the personal appeal and reach of a human hand." [1]

Parker, in contrast, had personal warmth. Quiet as his emotionality was he seems to have been always ready to help persons from any walk of life, and to have impressed them with the genuineness of his concrete concern for them. Although he wrote of his own childhood that "it was good to be brought up among religious Unitarians," he reported that, even then, these good people seemed too cold to him, and often failed to "do justice to simple religious feeling." The preaching of too many liberal ministers, he said, was

[1] John White Chadwick, *William Ellery Channing, Minister of Religion* (Boston: Houghton Mifflin, 1903), p. 363.

"related too much to outward things, not enough to the inward pious life." [2]

Here were two men, then, of first-rate mind and courage, exemplifying in common everything that was best in early Unitarianism, but in whom radically different types of personality led to radically different conceptions and implications in the actual practice of ministry.

With due respect to the tradition of Channing, with his great soaring thoughts, it is nevertheless my thesis that the tradition of Parker more deeply exemplifies the whole range of convictions of the liberal movement and that our concern today in such an area as pastoral care may look more to Parker than to Channing for direction in the conception of our role and function as ministers.

William Ellery Channing

William Ellery Channing possessed a mind both powerful and systematic. Unorthodox as his system and that of Unitarianism in his day might seem to be to the prevailing Calvinists, it was Channing perhaps above all who argued convincingly that the new system hung together.

I observe, then, that Unitarianism promotes piety because it is a rational religion. By this I do not mean that its truths can be fully comprehended; for there is not an object in nature or religion which has not innumerable connections and relations beyond our grasp of thought. I mean that its doctrines are consistent with one another, and with all established truth. [3]

[2] Frances Power Cobbe, ed., *The Collected Works of Theodore Parker* (London: Trübner and Co., 1865), 12, 311.

[3] *The Works of William E. Channing, D.D.*, with an introduction (New and complete ed., rearranged; Boston: American Unitarian Association, 1886), p. 398.

Channing was sensitively aware of the many dualities in human life, perhaps especially of the conflict between reason and emotion. The most important thing that can be said about man is that he can, through his mind and reason, rise above being improperly controlled by his emotions, that this same mind can read God's revelations (in the Bible but not confined to the Bible) and help man to move toward growth in virtue in the basic moral sense. Man is not, warned Channing, to permit his gifts of reason and cognition to be set aside in favor of some alleged supernatural or divine intrusion that makes mind worthless. Mind or reason is the God-conferred gift by which man can transcend his emotionality, including even his untrustworthiness or his depravity.

To Channing, God is "for man," so to speak, but for man by way of man's rational apprehensions of God's intent for man's growth in virtue. God is no arbitrary dictator, but a patient, persistent, and loving Creator who understands that the aim of all growth in virtue, love of God, is at the same time the highest growth of man's human potentiality as a creature. Thus, piety is never sufficient, although it is important. Religion is, thus, interrelated with life.

Believe in reason though he did, Channing nevertheless warned against any rationalism devoid of religious concern.

I apprehend that among those Christians who bear the name of rational, from the importance which they give to the exercise of reason in religion, love to Christ has lost something of its honor, in consequence of its perversion. It has too often been substituted for *practical* religion.[4]

Channing also said, "Men may be too rational as well as

[4] *Ibid.*, p. 322.

too fervent." [5] Thus, reason was indeed the main instrument to the improvement of man's lot, and to his moral development; but it was to be trusted only when it was set in the context of religious concern, of belief in a *pro nobis* Creator-God who has given and continues to give revelations which if appropriately understood help man to the aim that God intends, but does not dictate. There was indeed, in Channing, a theological system; and in what it asserted (laying aside perhaps what it tried to negate) it was closer to the long-term Christian tradition than Channing or any historical scholar of his period may have realized.

Channing perceived something of the conflict-ridden nature of actual human life, and none of his dualism was irrelevant. But because of the intellectual climate of his time and his own personality characteristics, he dealt abstractly with the dualisms and contradictions by a general method of opposing the "lower" with the "higher." Indeed, the fundamental function of the minister, from Channing's point of view, is to be advocate and interpreter of the higher, in order that the lower may have no controlling influence. The logic of this view drove Channing, at least in theory and in his ordination addresses, to recognize the importance of dealing with individual persons in all their actual duality. In ordination addresses he said:

Preaching is not your whole or chief work. Private intercourse is to you a more important instrument than the pulpit. You must not wait for the poor in the church. Go to them in their homes. Go where no other will go. Let no squalidness, or misery, or crime, repel you. Seek the friendless, the forsaken, the desponding, the lost. Penetrate the depths of poverty, the haunts of intemperance, the strongholds of sin. Feel an attrac-

[5] *Ibid.*, p. 254.

tion in what others shun, in the bleak room open to the winter's wind, in the wasted form and the haggard countenance, in the very degradation of your race.[6]

Even for the early nineteenth century the rhetoric is power-ful and compelling. But its injunction to concrete concern cannot conceal the fact that its thought is about abstracted types of human need. In the same address Channing con-tinued:

What weapon shall you take with you? You will be told to arm yourselves with caution, to beware of deception, to take the shield of prudence, and the breastplate of distrust. . . . This lesson is indeed important, . . . but prudence and caution are only defensive armor, . . . they give no power over misery, poverty, and vice. The real power is to be found in a *higher principle.*[7]

The persuasiveness of the rhetoric continues, and the in-junctions to courage and risk are timeless in their signifi-cance. But one wonders what the theological student who was being ordained actually felt about the "higher principle" when he had decided, in response to the speech, to frequent a saloon, make calls in the slums, and even make a visit at the prison?

Channing continued, also at an ordination address:

Your life is to be spent, not in retired study, but very much in visits from house to house; and this has its advantages. It will bring you near the poor, awaken your sympathies with them, acquaint you with their wants, and give them a confidence

[6] *Ibid.,* p. 90.
[7] *Ibid.*

in your attachment which will open their hearts to your public instructions.[8]

Despite the public-relations dimensions of this injunction, softening them up so they will come to hear you preach, the injunction itself is obviously genuine although dealing with classes of need, "the poor," for instance, and not with the individual desperation or apathy of concrete poverty.

Channing, however, was fundamentally wary of attachment to concrete need situations, as quite possibly diverting the young minister from his larger and higher concerns:

But it has, too, its disadvantages. There is danger that your mind may be frittered away by endless details, by listening continually to frivolous communications and suspicious complaints. To escape these narrowing influences, you should steadily devote a part of every day to solitary study; and, still more, you should make it your rule to regard the events and experiences of every day as lessons, and strive to extract from them general truths, so that the intellect may enlarge itself in the midst of the humblest concerns.[9]

A biographer of Channing described him as standing once in the midst of a bereaved and heartbroken family, and saying, no doubt with deepest sincerity, "What a mysterious Providence!" [10] Without denigrating the importance of generalizing from concrete instances of encounter, one can hardly escape the conclusion that Channing's self-admitted weakness before the individual made him uneasy about immersion in any concrete situation of need. He continued, in the address quoted above: "Every man is a novel, a

[8] *Ibid.*, p. 97.
[9] *Ibid.*
[10] Chadwick, *Channing*, p. 363.

volume, if you know how to read him. To seize the universal in the particular is the great art of wisdom, and this is especially important to one who is to live amidst details." [11]

Here we see the power of Channing's logical mind forcing him to acknowledge the priority of concreteness, the imagination of his appreciation for "system" leading to advocacy of proper generalization from concrete encounter, but the defensive, and perhaps even obsessional, fear of the consequences of emotional immersion as tending to disengagement, noninvolvement, the holding of empathy at arm's length.

Although Channing was not unappreciative of feeling and emotions, one wonders if he did not think of them as "those" or "that," rather than as "me" or "mine"? The very structure of the thought seems to make them "other," rather than aspects of "me" and of "life" that require attention as well as control. "What a mysterious Providence!" may not be an inappropriate self-reflection of a minister even in the midst of an encounter with deeply and starkly bereaved persons. It is surely far superior to "God must have his reasons for this death," or to "It's all crazy." But if the minister generalizes *too soon*, then he is under suspicion of defending himself against very human feelings of empathy, whose very presence are somehow inwardly threatening. Channing was, I think, inwardly afraid of such involvements. And in full justice to his greatness, it would seem that his own self-appraisal was not unaware of the actual situation.

Channing was brilliant, courageous, far from unaware of his own one-sidedness, and a deeply (if disengagedly) religious man. But his semiobsessionalism rendered him, at the central point of our concern, an unsafe guide for the future.

[11] *The Works of Channing,* p. 97.

Admonitory prudence, while not irrelevant, is not the first principle of pastoral care.

Theodore Parker

Parker, like Channing, believed in "system," in pulling together the insights about relationships, rather than letting them sit, individually, in various corners in unrelated fashion. His system was, however, more "open," perhaps most importantly in its spirit and attitude. Parker lived only fifty years; he died in 1860. Had he lived thirty years longer, the whole course of Unitarianism might have been changed.

Late in his life of only a half century, Parker wrote a book-length letter to his congregation, entitled *Experience as a Minister*. The very writing of this document, to say nothing of its title, is characteristic of Parker, and suggests the contrast with Channing, who would never have written such a letter, and who, if he had, would have called it something like *The Church and the World* or *Moral Progress Under God Through Reason and Responsibility*.

In this letter as well as in other writings Parker showed the simplicity of his basic categories. At least in some respects, his mind was perhaps not so penetrating as Channing's, especially in regard to the function of any set of categories. But even his categories were unassailable for what they tried to demonstrate. They were: God, Man, Religion. In the letter he dealt with the first under the title "The Infinite Perfection of God"; with the second under the heading "The Adequacy of Man for All His Functions"; and on the third with a straw-man question, "Absolute or Natural Religion?"

Parker was certainly attentive to the holistic interpretation of creation in the Christian tradition:

In its complete and perfect form, this is the normal development, use, discipline, and enjoyment of every part of the body, and every faculty of the spirit; the direction of all natural powers to their natural purposes.[12]

Religion was for fulfillment in life. Here, to be sure, the eighteenth century speaks on "nature," with a convenient setting-aside of aggression and blood and exploitation; but here speaks also the holism of the creation stories in the biblical book of Genesis. If more sophistication is inserted into the term natural, then every Christian theologian today would go along with the Parker statement.

God, to Parker, was no mere human construct, no mere hypothesis to be put together on the basis of man's reflections. God was, just as in Calvinism, almighty, omniscient, unlimited in his conscience or knowledge of good and evil, and also unlimited in his love and hence omnigracious. God, with all his power and wisdom, was also "for man." Perhaps most important of all, God was integrated within himself; all these characteristics fit together in God; in him there was no contradiction.

To Parker, God was immanent in the world of matter and the world of Spirit, and these two realms, understood in Parker's terms, were exhaustive of reality. In the former realm Parker saw God effecting his purposes with or without human aid. But in the realm of the Spirit he saw God's fulfillment of his aims as resting upon needed cooperation on man's part. In some basic way the fulfillment of God's ends is partly dependent upon man. Thus there is a basic partnership between God and man.

Man's life as man is to fulfill the purpose of God for his life, since that purpose is man's proper fulfillment. God

[12] Cobbe, *The Works of Parker*, pp. 297-98.

has laid out the pattern, and shown it through his revelations. It is up to man to make the plan a reality, both because it is God's intent and because that intent is man's fulfillment. And, empirical as he was when he felt empiricism relevant, Parker confessed honestly the *a priori* nature of this kind of belief:

It is not difficult in this general way to show the relative perfection of Human Nature, deducing this from the Infinite Perfection of God; but I think it impossible to prove it by the inductive process of reasoning from concrete facts of external observation, of which we know not yet the entire sum, nor any one, perhaps, completely.[13]

In a related statement Parker argued for the dignity of man's mind and his personality, but always with the background of implicit impact of God upon man:

I have travelled also this inductive road, as far as it reaches, and tried to show the constitution of man's Body, with its adaptation to the surrounding world of matter, and the constitution of man's Spirit, with its intellectual, moral, affectional, and religious powers, and its Harmonious Relation with the world of matter, which affords them a playground, a school, and a workshop . . . I have taught that man has in himself all the faculties he needs to accomplish his high destination, and in the world of matter finds, one by one, all the material help he requires.[14]

How Parker would have responded to the ambiguous creative-destructive potentialities of atomic energy, we have no notion. No doubt he would have accentuated the positive potential. He did say: "We all see the Unity of Life in the

[13] *Ibid.*, p. 296.
[14] *Ibid.*

56

Individual; his gradual growth from merely sentient and passive babyhood, up to thoughtful self-directing manhood." [15]

Parker certainly saw in his pastoral experience all kinds of people who did not make it to thoughtful self-directing manhood. But his main concern was to manifest such a goal as normative for human beings, under God. Parker was on the edge of modern developmental conceptions, but he never crossed the border. Both God's benevolent plan for man, and man's pursuit of (or retreat from) that plan, are almost but never quite viewed dynamically.

True religion, to Parker, was seen categorically in three parts: emotional, intellectual, and practical. Religion, in racial history, was felt to begin in man's primal instincts, eventually leading, under proper influence, to "right feelings." The intellectual part consisted of "true ideas, which either directly represent the primitive, instinctive feeling of whoso holds them, or else produce a kindred, secondary and derivative feeling in whoso receives them." From the modern point of view, this statement is astonishing in its refusal, finally, to yield to a compartmentalized faculty psychology. Whatever "intellect" may be, it is not to be regarded as divorced from life and feeling.

Parker's third part was the practical part, relating to "just and correct action," or the moral and relational consequences of true religion. Important as are emotion and intellect, Parker declared that man's actual salvation, if it comes, is through the third part, through moral and just and correct action and relationships. "What good is not with us is before, to be attained by Toil, and Thought, and Religious Life." [16]

[15] *Ibid.*
[16] *Ibid.*, p. 298.

The issuance of true religion into just and correct action was, as Parker saw it, more appropriately stressed by Unitarians than by any others. But Parker did not believe, all the same, that if the action were just and correct nothing else mattered. He was as much against the "corpse-cold Unitarianism of Harvard College and Brattle Street" as was Ralph Waldo Emerson, the framer of the phrase.[17] He deplored the lack of deep, internal feelings of piety among many Unitarians; and he called such feelings that "most joyous of all delights." Let preaching indeed be to the "understanding, the conscience, and the will." But let it be also to the soul. "Duty, Duty! Work, Work!" are needed indeed, but equally important is, "Joy, Joy! Delight, Delight!" Parker wrote about the "cold" Unitarians:

Their vessels were full of water; it was all laboriously pumped up from deep wells; it did not gush out, leaping from the Great Spring, that is indeed on the surface of the sloping ground, feeling the little streams that run among the hills, and both quenching the wild asses' thirst and watering also the meadows newly mown, but which yet comes from the Rock of Ages, and is pressed out by the Cloud-compelling mountains that rest thereon—yes, by the gravitation of the earth itself.[18]

If only, sometimes, Unitarians could be "wild asses," Parker pined.

Parker's openness demanded not only that he take a new look at the possible discrepancies between Unitarian aspirations and Unitarian orthodoxy, but also that he reexamine the orthodox Christian traditions (especially Calvinism) for possible truths whatever the orthodox (and the Calvinists)

[17] *Ibid.*, p. 297.
[18] *Ibid.*, p. 312.

might have made out of them. The basic trouble with the Calvinism of his day, Parker felt, was in its exclusivist stress upon the greatness and dreadfulness of God, with too little noted about God's love, his concern for man's fulfillment, and his grace. By the same token, only the depravity of man was emphasized, and not also the beautiful dimension of man. He was partly nostalgic in his reexamination of the possible truths in Calvinism; he knew quite well that some of the New England Calvinistic piety of his day was, ideas aside, precisely what he was arguing for in Unitarianism. While out of sympathy with some of the prevailing Calvinistic ideas—"old ecclesiastic Supernaturalism, that with its whip of fear yet compelled a certain direct, though perverted, action of the simple religious element in the Trinitarians" [19]—he yet saw their virtues too. But he was finally out of sympathy with the kind of "coldness" many of them had even as he was with the different kind of "coldness" among his Unitarian colleagues.

Although both were revered leaders and prophetic voices, Parker far more than Channing prevented Unitarianism from becoming fixed in particular points of conviction, belief, and practice. Spontaneous and creative developments in and by man, he felt, needed to be attended to, supported, and put in their proper theological context. Here, it may be said, was not only Parker's kinship with the universal-hero motif, but also with the dynamic character of Christian revelation itself.

Parker's actual influence upon subsequent Unitarian modes of thought and action was considerable. But it was selective and partial. Parker's openness, for instance, was attended to

[19] *Ibid.*

when certain novel ideas were appearing; but it was not followed either in a reexamination of Calvinism or in an appraisal of Freud's revelations about the depths of aggression in human life. Real openness is never an insurance policy against shock; either in face of the novel revelation or of the reexamination of the truth of the old or discarded.

In summary, Parker conceived the basic function of the ministry in educational terms. It was the minister's first job to stimulate the progressive development of his people toward the highest faculties of which they were capable; and indeed to the extent that this task was pursued it would also extend beyond the people of the parish and would influence, educationally speaking, the people of the larger community. If persons could truly grasp the meaning of their moral and spiritual responsibility within the context both of their organic nature and their social relationships, then moral action would become not mere duty but also love and feeling and concern, and would also contribute to the betterment of the body communal.

In rather fancy language to our ears, but with the ring of authenticity, Parker's biographer, O. B. Frothingham, attests to Parker's "pastoral concern" as including a quiet, nonaggressive, but very deep, attentiveness to real people in real situations:

Those of his parish in West Roxbury he stimulated to study by giving them his precious time, correcting their attempts at composition in the most attractive way. "Don't write about nightingales, my child: listen to the robin and the bluebird in our fields." [20]

[20] Octavius Brooks Frothingham, *Theodore Parker: A Biography* (Boston: James R. Osgood and Co., 1874), p. 245.

Let imagination proceed from experience, and not be a fantasy substitute for it.

Nor did he wait for their application, but with exploring kindness sought out those whom he could help, and gave aid in the spirit so brotherly that it could not be refused. The president of Harvard College had a standing request to let him know of any deserving youth whom a little money would help. He counted it a privilege to pay the bills of an incipient scholar.[21]

Now that Harvard's endowment has passed the billion-dollar mark, it is not clear how the current director of financial aid would look upon a Parker-like offer, especially when the student was supposed to emerge as some kind of scholar, a fate regarded as worse than death by most current Harvard men. But then, Parker's was a simpler age, and perhaps Harvard was too.

No devotion to his studies ever led him to disregard an appeal for assistance, from whatever quarter. He never seemed to feel that there were any rights he had which man, woman, or child, black or white, was bound to respect, but voluntarily tied himself hand and foot, and laid himself smiling on the altar of self-sacrifice. Just as he might be pouring out on paper the full flow of his thoughts a tap at the library door, answered by the ready, "Come!" would bring in some unknown visitor. The pen was quietly dipped into the cup; the India cane chair slipped round from the desk to the sofa, where the comer was invited to sit; while the genial, "What can I do for you?" uttered as quietly as if no torrent had been checked in its course, put the two in harmonious relations.[22]

Whether Parker had more, in the harmonious relations,

[21] *Ibid.*
[22] *Ibid.*

61

than attentiveness, concern, and good intentions, we do not know. Certainly even he did not have available the insights that have emerged from modern scientific study. But even that study has shown that the concern, the attentiveness, the ability to focus right now on concreteness and person, are the indispensable resources and background of all true pastoral care, whatever may be needed in addition.

As a kind of orthodox Unitarianism developed, there was opposition both to Parker's conception of freedom of inquiry in religion—including reexamination of the old as well as attentiveness to the new whether you liked it or not—and to his practice of taking the fully concrete human situation with utmost attentive seriousness. On the latter point, Channing's concern for general truth was sometimes, unhappily, quoted against the Parker emphasis.

Even Parker did not have, I am sure, the insights we need for ministry today. But his spirit, his personality, his openness, and his conception of openness seem to me to provide a background utterly consistent with the Unitarian tradition, on which a new concern for pastoral care may be built today.

If we do, in fact, succeed in getting some appropriate pastoral care into the Unitarian Universalist churches, our historical debt will be greatest to Theodore Parker. But even he cannot supply the details of what we need for today.

People

Both Channing and Parker were concerned about people, and both were Jewish, Christian, and human enough to be concerned about them in the whole range of their experience: diet and sex and worship and healing and war and crime and race and beauty and fulfillment. Being nineteenth-century men, both concentrated in their theoretical statements on the ideals, on what ought to be and might be in fact. Both were Christians without apology, and Unitarians with reasons attached. Both had great influence upon the subsequent development of Unitarianism, and both were influential beyond this group.

Both Channing and Parker have, unhappily, fallen out of fashion, except perhaps for a few history-minded Unitarians. This fact is unfortunate, especially about Parker. Our analysis has tried to show that, although Parker's specific categories may indeed not do for today, his fundamental insights lead in the direction of a pastoral obligation for pastoral care that can not lightly be set aside. We do not believe that Channing, abstract as he was, was against this, but only that he was afraid of it.

We suggest, then, that liberalism of today read properly the message from both Channing and Parker; that Channing's concern be interpreted in the context of his defensiveness and his fear; and that Parker's more comprehensive outlook become the historical base from which present-day ministers of the liberal persuasion look upon their pastoral task. Parker does not tell us everything we need to know; such a thought would have been as alien to him as it is to us. But he had not only the idea, but also the approach, the concern, and the theoretical underpinning that linked the concrete encounter with the larger dimensions of ministry.

CONTEMPORARY LIBERAL MINISTERS' ATTITUDES TOWARD PASTORAL CARE

Carl E. Wennerstrom and Seward Hiltner

For this chapter and the next, all the data were secured by Carl Wennerstrom through interviews with about ten Unitarian Universalist ministers. The interviews were recorded with the consent of the ministers. Except for the typist who transcribed the tapes and Jeanne Wennerstrom, who examined this material after her husband's death, no one has seen these interview reports except Seward Hiltner, who wrote this chapter on the basis of the Wennerstrom transcribed interviews. If Carl Wennerstrom had lived to write up and interpret the interview material, he would probably have felt much more free to present long quotations to indicate aspects of the minister's attitudes toward pastoral care. For my part, it seems important, for ethical reasons, to lean toward reporting little rather than much. Knowing a good deal about Carl Wennerstrom's mind and his convictions, it is my earnest effort to interpret the material that follows as I believe he would have done.

Since I do not feel free to use lengthy quotations from the ministers, or to present even disguised versions of cases they had dealt with and which they reported confidentially to Carl Wennerstrom, I shall employ two devices which aid in interpreting the material but which eliminate any possible chance of identification of any minister. The four paradoxical characteristics of liberal ministers, rationalism, reformism, dramatics, and distance, were offered in the first chapter by Carl Wennerstrom as dynamic reasons for the present-day situation in pastoral care by liberal ministers. Armed with these, in this chapter I have examined all the interview materials, and have presented some short and not identifiable quotations that demonstrate, in most instances, the presence of the characteristics Wennerstrom noted, but in other instances some transcendence of those characteristics so far as they are limitations. The next chapter will present a kind of case.

As a part of most of his long interviews, Carl Wennerstrom asked the ministers to engage in a role-playing situation with him. Each minister was simply to be himself and to do his best. Wennerstrom began with the same basic situation in each instance. He tried—and he was an artist at it—to read himself fully into the role he was portraying, and with which each minister in turn tried to deal. The reports of these role-played interviews are fascinating. The range of insight and ability thereby demonstrated was fairly wide among the ten ministers. Statistical handling of them would be meaningless. But there was one role-played interview which Wennerstrom regarded as superior to the others. Though not perfect, it was very good, because it both manifested clearly all the characteristics (rationalism, reformism, dramatics, and distance) identified as partial impediments, and yet, at the same time, demonstrated how in the hands of this minister each characteristic by itself and all of them jointly were used in the interest of effective pastoral care.

The interview showed too how the characteristics were set aside when not relevant to the helping task. As has been done in my reporting of this role-playing situation, Carl Wennerstrom would certainly have offered discriminating comment on various aspects of the performance. But both in terms of attitude and insight demonstrated, and in terms of showing the direction that pastoral care by liberal ministers may take without departure from liberal convictions, there seems no doubt that this instance was as close as Wennerstrom got to a "model." The write-up here is abbreviated but is otherwise faithful to the tape recording. It has also been looked over by the minister who participated in the interview with Carl Wennerstrom, and he has approved both its content and its publication, and has offered a helpful critique. Responsibility for interpretative comments is of course wholly mine.

Characteristics of the Liberal Paradox in Pastoral Care

The four characteristic elements of the paradox have been identified as rationalism, reformism, dramatics, and distance. Wennerstrom felt that, although these elements are interrelated, they are of increasing importance in the order stated, i.e., distance was more important than dramatics, dramatics, more important than reformism, and reformism, more important than rationalism. In a rough-and-ready way the interview materials tend to confirm this order of significance, judging both from the number of statements that can obviously be classed under each and also from the importance assigned by the men themselves to such statements (although of course without benefit of the categories). We shall consider these elements in turn.

Rationalism. Although rationalism, even in the sense of Channing, is probably not entirely dead among Unitarians, and liberals in general, neither its content nor context have remained unaffected by the wars and revolutions and discoveries of this century, and by the views of Freud, Marx, and many other seminal thinkers.

Insofar as rationalism is simply the absence of an "irrationalism" that refuses to think or to do much else but cling, then of course reason is prominent in these interviews; but on such a point there would be virtually no difference with conservative or right-wing ministers of today. On the other side, if rationalism were identified as a declaration of the controlling powers of intellect over feeling, body, organic processes, and concrete relationships, then it seems clear that none of our liberal ministers is rationalist in such a sense.

There are in the interview materials, however, two senses in which at least some of the ministers demonstrate something that seems to be in the liberal rationalistic tradition. One is illustrated by the minister who said of his efforts in pastoral counseling, "My chief endeavor is to get people to want less in order that they might get more and be happy with the situation." This is a kind of counsel of prudence, a rational-moral variant of Stoic principles, perhaps even a kind of lower-case Philistinism. The strong moral preoccupation behind this kind of rationalism (indeed, its never-quite-successful attempt to transcend duty) is further demonstrated in the same minister's statement, "You're only required to do what you're required to do. . . . If I do my part and some guy utterly flubs it, that's his fault and not mine. . . . I'm thus far able to discharge my own conscience."

The proximity of this kind of rationalism to Stoicism

in the ancient world, and to existentialism in the modern world, is shown in this statement from a minister: "All that man loves perishes. To my mind, that is the beginning of wisdom. You can't make peace with death if you can't make peace with life. This is a principle that underlies my pastoral counseling . . . (but) I can't get anyone to pay attention to it." Here are surely courage, insight, and concern, as well as a strict attempt at intellectual honesty. This is in no way an arid or cerebral rationalism. But its last line, the plaint of those who will not heed truth, reveals its rationalistic flavor in the Stoical or existentialist sense.

The other form of rationalism that appears in the interviews might be called "developmental" rather than "moral-existential." The liberal, said one minister, has "both the right and the obligation to develop his theology," and he should understand that the church "offers him freedom and fellowship together." He "is free on the condition that he grants other people the right to be free." By implication, the fellowship supports his freedom in the sense indicated and also encourages him to "develop his theology" as his own way of thinking and understanding.

This developmental rationalism also appears in the minister who advocated, in the light of the liberal principle of "freedom to think," a "confirmation" ceremony (with emphasis on the preparation for it) that would confirm not faith as particular beliefs but doubt as the immediate experience of "freedom to think." The "naturalness of doubting" should be stressed, he added.

When, in the instance of a couple of the ministers, these modern forms of liberal rationalism—moral, existential, and developmental—had been filtered through some explicit training in pastoral care and counseling, the aptness of any kind of rationalism designation becomes problematical. One minister said, when discussing a person in a particular pastoral situation, "Rather than trying to get through to him on an intellectual level, I tried to get through to him on an emotional level, by accepting his feelings, especially his despair and his discouragement. In this way I hoped that he could bring all these elements together and regain his wholeness."

A few of the liberal ministers interviewed, like some of their brothers toward the center and right of the theological spectrum, presented a cryptic rationalism under the guise of moralism that took a black-and-white view of many concrete moral situations. But even they did not advocate conquest of emotion by intellect, even though they underestimated the difficulty of guiding moral decision by knowledge of truth and commitment to right.

For the most part, however, the conclusion is inescapable that contemporary liberal ministers, Unitarians in particular, are very much members of the world of modern thought and, with rare exceptions, do not believe in any simple priority of mind over emotion as the key to life's problems and potentialities. The conclusion may also be drawn therefore, that rationalism in its older forms is as dead here as it is among centrist and right-wing theological ministers.

But it is also the conclusion that what I have called the moral-existentialist and the developmental forms of rationalism are part of the background furniture, or mental assumptions, of most liberal ministers today (to the extent that our brief sample is in any way representative). Since most readers like myself will feel warm sympathy for these categories of moral-existential and developmental, so long as the pejorative word *rationalism* is not associated with them, they will probably protest the association of the latter

69

word with the adjectives. Are these really forms of rationalism?

Readers may be reminded that Carl Wennerstrom's use
of this term was as paradox and not as simple pejoration.
If the presence of *ism* after any word at all connotes un-
relieved negativity, then the *moral-existential* and the *developmental* somethings that have been discussed could not
be rational*isms*. But if the "ism" is handled more lightly,
and with more attention to ambiguity, then even rationalism
may be conceded enough ambiguity to qualify as paradox.
This seems to have been the intent of Carl Wennerstrom.

Wennerstrom was clearly in favor of some things in what
I have called the moral-existential and the developmental
aspects of liberal rationalism. But, if these are really paradoxes, he was just as clearly against other aspects.

The positive aspect of moral-existential rationalism lies
in its combination of realistic perception, courageous
confrontation, and responsible action in the light of
perception and confrontation. Its negative aspects, however,
inhere in its tendency toward a "bootstrap theology," in
which one pulls himself up from his existential mousehood
to his appropriate manhood by his own perceptual accuracy,
emotional courage, and moral perseverance. Carl Wennerstrom's clinical experience made him wary on this point,
although it was always nice work if you could get it.

The positive aspect of developmental rationalism lies in
its penetrating vision of the dialectical relationship between
faith and doubt, and between life and interpretation of life.
It knows (and it is correct) that real faith is always on
some kind of boundary line, or else it is protecting itself
from encounter with whatever faith should be meeting.
The negative aspect of developmental rationalism is, however, equally real. Some doubt is obsessional, and would

be "embarrassed" rather than resolved by faith. It is fine to be skeptical or questioning a lot of the time, or aware of what one does not know, or even "heuristic," as scientists like to generalize it. But you can not, generally speaking, aid your marriage by coming home and looking at your wife in a mood of doubt, even of a heuristic kind, unless you believe in reincarnation and wonder who can get along with her the next time round.

If I have correctly understood Carl Wennerstrom about rationalism, and correctly interpreted what his minister-interviewees said to him that bears on this point, then the good news lies in the form in which rationalism now appears: more sophisticated, more subtle, more sensitive to the whole personality (and hence to the Jewish-Christian doctrine about creation) than in the previous century. But there is still danger even in these versions of rationalism. Although deepened insights are in their achievement and their thrust great stuff, their possessors may become victims of "pride," try to treat their wives or children or even the self like laboratory experiments, or overlook, in the developmental pilgrimage, the fact that doubt no less than faith may have its pathologies.

Reformism. Virtually every one of the ministers interviewed by Carl Wennerstrom was, or had been, or would be, chairman, president, secretary, program director, or even official agitator of organizations in the community, state, and nation, representing causes that no thoughtful citizen could be against unless he were of the extreme right, or left, wing, speaking politically, economically, racially, or internationally. In other words, the causes in which the ministers had invested themselves beyond their parish boundaries, and the organizations necessary to support those causes, were what 90 percent of our citizens, so far as they had considered the issues at all, would regard as worth appropriate concern. Very many of the causes have no political angles at all. Mental deficiency is neither Democratic nor Republican, conservative nor liberal. Neither is disaster-relief, or funds for research about the heart, or programs to foster mental health. In other words, many of the social causes have no social enemies but extremists so far as goals are concerned. Others, of course, have enemies not only on specific methods but also on the very nature of the goals.

I was astonished to find in the Wennerstrom interviews with ministers very little about approaching the world through reformism; especially so, since I have some knowledge of the monumental work done by Unitarians in particular and religious liberals in general in fostering reform causes over the past century, and with particular reference to the kinds of causes where imagination about how to get, and enthusiasm in getting, something done took precedence over controversy about the goal. Here, the recognition of complexity apparently affects liberals as well as others even though in Unitarians it does not lead to a "failure of nerve" about trying what can be tried. Perhaps this nobility about participation and leadership and realism about possible consequences stem from Channing and Parker, neither of whom alleged much about saving the world in one generation.

The reformism tendency in Unitarian history, as Carl Wennerstrom saw it, tended on the positive side to attack general problem areas, mostly with effectiveness; but on the negative side it sometimes neglected the immediate and pressing particularity of need. In the gross form of this statement there is no evidence that that trend, especially on the negative side, continues into the present. The reader of the Wennerstrom interviews is a bit alarmed, on the one hand, with the paucity of comments about how this or that bit of social action (on mental health, mental deficiency, racial matters, and the like) will eventually prevent some problems from arising. It may be that even Unitarians are having a temporary failure of nerve about preventing some social ills. On the other hand, the evidence from the interviews about attendance to or neglect of particular and pressing need is generally reassuring. Even the ministers who do counseling only when pressed, nevertheless do it; and with their sophistication, do not take refuge in denying need short of murder or suicide. Still, a number of them are not overly happy with a world in which they have to try to pick up the pieces. At least by implication, they would prefer a more clean-cut world in which reformism could create appropriate and effective helping resources. But perhaps unlike some of their predecessors, most Unitarian ministers today seem not preoccupied with that possibility, at least as a substitute for trying to help the poeple who actually come to them right now.

Most of the ministers interviewed by Carl Wennerstrom knew, at least in their heads, that telling people what to do would not work, that listening was essential, that the immediate aims of pastoral care with this person or that should be related to the situation from which the relationship began, and the like. And yet most of them still reserved, at least in their private opinions expressed to Wennerstrom, the right to judge where the person ought to move, provided it could be managed. Perhaps this is the pastoral heritage of reformism.

One minister said, "I think most of my people fall far short of the implied measure, the measure implied in their own natures, and what I want to do is kick them in the seat of the pants." His way of kicking, however, was demonstrated as generally prudent.

Another minister, noting in his community what he felt was a kind of adult consent to a considerable number of teen-age pregnancies out of the marriage relationship, felt that the community mores were "too much to tackle for any one individual," and he also felt that collaboration by himself and other community leaders was likely to have no constructive influence. Such an attitude seems to move by the failure-of-nerve route away from reformism. Early Unitarians would also have been shocked at the declaration by another minister, "I engage in community activities because it's my obligation."

Yet another minister quoted in the Wennerstrom interview a phrase from Stuart Chase, "Let there be an end to oughtness." As his further discussion suggested, he interpreted this phrase as negative to social and ethical obligation when viewed as conformity to anything outside, whereas movement from one's own nature would not be "oughtness" in the impositional sense. Not enough information was given to show whether this minister's attitude was simply an ethical revision in the light of psychological wisdom, or was instead a kind of romanticism. In either event, however, it was not very close to reformism.

In a rough and ready way, the degree of reformism (in the sense defined in the first chapter) that became evident in the interviews seemed to be correlated with the age of the particular minister; i.e., the older the minister, the more reformist. If this should be true, in any degree, even with many exceptions (and general observation suggests it could not possibly be true of liberal ministers without a large number of evident exceptions), a serious exploration of its meaning and significance would have to go far beyond the limited aims of the present discussion. From the point of view of our concern, however, it could suggest that liberal ministers, whether they all like it or not, are compelled to spend more time than formerly on patchwork jobs (pastoral care and counseling) and less on trying to construct new helping resources. Thus in a sociological sense they are more like other ministers.

From the point of view of Wennerstrom's thesis, it seems clear that more liberal ministers are spending more time in pastoral care, but also that some of this increased time is given reluctantly and on two grounds; first, reluctance about the activity itself; and second, reluctance about the time thus not made available for larger causes. The present status of reformism is, therefore, not simple, but this analysis does tend to suggest the appropriateness of paradox as applied to it.

Dramatics. Going through the interview material from the perspective of Wennerstrom's insights into dramatics has clearly tended to confirm the significance of the insight. The dramatics have manifested themselves in several ways.

Fairly early in most of the interviews, Wennerstrom asked each minister to give him (confidentially, of course) one or more instances with which he had actually dealt in his pastoral care and counseling, sometimes making the suggestion about marriage counseling (hardly any counseling can exclude a marital and family angle). A considerable number of the cases actually cited by the ministers were, in the most obvious sense of the term, dramatic in character: the near-divorce, the almost-suicide, even anonymous name-dropping, "If I mentioned the name, it would be widely known." Although the cases offered covered a wide range of content, the majority of them focused around the making of some crucial decision. In this sense, most of them were "action cases," i.e., dramatic cases. This is very far from saying that these ministers jumped in naïvely, or took decision out of their parishioners' hands. Even the ministers less well trained in pastoral care exhibited great respect for the autonomy of the persons they were trying to help. But for most of them, what seemed to make a situation interesting was the presence of the need for decision, whether the person was actually helped to get round to the decision or not.

One minister, while demonstrating real respect for the autonomy of his people, nevertheless (in casual side remarks) saw his pastoral-care function as being an umpire, as patching up a situation, and as going "one step beyond permissiveness" in his work. Perhaps the underlying dynamics of this kind of concern are illuminated by the minister frank enough to say, "I just don't like weak people." Weak people are presumably violating the rules of the freedom game; i.e., I respect your autonomy, so what decision are you going to make with it? Dramatics may regret the content of the decision but respects decisiveness. Dramatics seems uncomfortable with ambiguity and indecisiveness. One minister, confronted with an instance of continuing indecision, articulated to the person that not to make a decision, for the time being, was a decision. This tactic may well have been relevant and helpful in the actual situation. But it also shows the dramatic decision-preoccupied discomfort in the face of continuing ambiguity or indecisiveness.

On occasion dramatics got into counseling methods. One minister with considerable insight into psychodynamics was asked by a woman to let her talk without interruption for an hour. He agreed but made a note on a slip of paper, turned it upside down on the table before him, listened without comment for the entire period, then turned up the slip and showed it to his parishioner. It read, "She wants to talk about committing suicide." In this instance, it seems his X-ray vision was correct. To say the least, his use of it was dramatic.

The covered-wagon, dig-your-own-wells aspect of dramatics, which Wennerstrom felt to be so close to the heart of the matter, was well illustrated by the minister who, expressing skepticism about the amount of interest in counseling that liberal ministers should take, said, "When everybody's jumping on the bandwagon, it seems to me that there must be a new step somewhere."

Another minister said, "I never read a book unless I've got a typewriter in front of me." He explained that this procedure was not so much for making notes on the book as for carrying through at once a notation of anything arising in his own mind in response to the reading, a quick on-paper reminder of any gem of thought "that's my own." Commendable as all this doubtless is, it confirms the Wennerstrom theory about dramatics. What is important is not what the book itself says, but the responsive and original thought set up in me. New wells are dug even under acknowledged oases.

In most but not all ministers, dramatics seems tempered by training and experience in actually helping people. There is in virtually all instances recognition of the wisdom of referring some people to psychiatric resources. And yet dramatics appears in the absence of any comment about referrals to social workers, who are, in fact, often best equipped to deal with complicated family tangles. The reason? Psychiatry is dramatic; social work is not.

The overall impression I get reinforces Wennerstrom's analysis of the predilection for dramatics among liberal ministers. Only among the less well trained (in pastoral care) does this tendency seem negatively to affect actual approach and method in concrete helping situations. For most of the ministers, the kind of situation apt to be affected by dramatics is the one they are most attentive to, the one they tend to be struck by and to remember, and the one that makes them feel, when they deal with it (whatever their success), that they are most properly being ministers.

None of the ministers who was interviewed admittedly evaded trying to help people in need, or denied that in his role of minister there were occasional bits of pseudo-psychiatry used but never consciously adopted as such. Even if the minister sees most pastoral care and counseling as patchwork and secretly wishes that a better world and stronger people would cut down the quantity of need for it, he regards it as a part of his ministry, does it conscientiously, and in most instances seems to have made a real stab at learning whatever he believes will help him to do it better (for some men, excluding the obvious kinds of training).

For the most part, however, the interviews show that the minister becomes truly involved and interested in pastoral care only when it becomes dramatic, i.e., when decision ought to be involved (whether in fact the person ever comes to decision or not). No cases were cited that focused on sustaining persons for whom "decision" would not possibly alter the overall situation. The sole case about death that was cited focused on confrontation of the reality. No case was mentioned involving, for instance, gradual and ambiguous adjustment to a permanent handicap. Nor were there any alcoholics, who appear naïvely

78

unambiguous at certain cross-sectional points but always come back with new levels of ambiguity. In short, inspection of the interview materials seems to reinforce altogether Carl Wennerstrom's insight into dramatics and pastoral care among liberal ministers.

Distance. Carl Wennerstrom's thesis about distance was that liberals like to be decisively helpful in the fashion of surgery, and feel uncomfortable when the relevant mode of helping is more like internal medicine with its ambiguous trying of this and then that and with no prior assurance that the involvement in real suffering will have, at any particular and predictable time, a decisive outcome. He did not believe that liberals are "cold." He thought them, rather, fearful of actual encounters with human suffering where both process and outcome are ambiguous; and hence, where the commitment has to be unremittingly to person, and not at all to decision. He thought them to be, however unwittingly, wary of genuine involvement without the support of probable movement toward decisiveness.

One minister said that "personal problems" as he began his ministry "flooded in upon me" in a measure he had not anticipated, so that he sought other sources of help from the start. As his ministry went on, he continued, he found that he was always carrying "in my pocket" some pastoral problem. No doubt other ministers would describe how they carried pastoral problems with the use of other metaphors: over the heart, in the mind, on the conscience, at the back of the head, or in the viscera. The pocket is, however useful, some kind of walling-off device. It is distant.

Another minister declared that the "pastoral job has to take into account the distinction between people who are basically sick and those who are not sick." He continued,

"My pastoral job is successful when I'm dealing with people who are basically healthy, who want to explore their values." The readiness of a person to explore values seems to imply his prior capacity to accept a certain distance, i.e., he will articulate contradictory pulls and impulses and ideals, and not mix them up ambiguously. The content of the discussion will clearly be more important than the relationship of the person.

Another minister of admirable honesty said, "I don't do much counseling, and I don't do any more than I have to." This man is by no means insensitive or without wisdom and devotion to the people he serves. He adds that quite often he finds himself "thinking in relation to somebody's problem," but that his meditations go on to the recognition "that it's more than just *his* problem." Here, one would guess, is a pastor who truly broods over the tangible Jerusalem situation, but who feels a little guilty about being so close to the specific problem that he can justify his intense concern only by readjusting the specific situation into a type, with statistical consequences that afford distance.

One minister cited the instance of a parishioner who found out that he had a fatal illness not long after the minister had preached a sermon on confronting terminal illness. The parishioner turned out to have "tremendous guts"; in other words, he had the attitude recommended in the sermon. "We lived through his terminal days together," said the minister. All this sounds most admirable. But strangely enough it seems to guarantee distance from ambiguity or uncertainty in a way that is not psychologically different from the old-fashioned, authoritarian clergyman's dealing with a parishioner with great depth of faith.

One minister carried the distance idea a step further to the need for "getting yourself off your hands." Until he had learned to do that, he said, his education and his ministry were unfulfilled. The phrase quoted may of course mean many things; but in context the impression given is of distance from critical self-reflection.

Another minister, perhaps with similar dynamics, complained that there are too many ministers too much involved in counseling; they are not "able to let the thing alone," he said. The implication of his remarks was: of course you have to do it sometimes, but keep your distance unless necessity compels it.

Distance too, in Wennerstrom's thought, is a category of paradox and not of simple negativity. It seems abundantly evident on both sides in the interviews with ministers, almost precisely as Wennerstrom described it in the first chapter.

A (PARTIAL) MODEL FOR LIBERAL PASTORAL CARE

*Carl E. Wennerstrom
and
Seward Hiltner*

The role that Carl Wennerstrom played in part of his interviews with most of the ministers saw him as an attractive, unmarried career woman of thirty-two, who wants to discuss with the minister her desire to have a baby out of wedlock by artificial insemination. We shall call the minister whose dealing with Carl Wennerstrom in his role is being reported, Mr. Cartwright; and the young woman (always Carl Wennerstrom in the role), Miss Davis. All dialogue is as it was transcribed from the tape, except for some patched syntax. Where material is omitted to make the report brief enough for a single chapter, the omission is noted. All interspersed comments of interpretation are by Seward Hiltner.

Carl Wennerstrom's opening description of Miss Davis was as follows: "Assume that a young woman of thirty-two comes to you. She has heard you preach; and in terms of that hearing, she believes that you may have something to offer her by way of counsel or advice on the problem that she brings. You learn from her opening statement of explanation that she is unmarried and that she is well-off financially. She has a good job as a professional woman, and she has also done well with investments.

"She goes on to tell you that she has been thinking of how biology may influence religious life, and she believes that she has an ethical problem along those lines. She says that she wants your help in relation to it. She has heard and read, she says further, about artificial insemination and has sounded out a physician on the prospect of his applying it to her despite her being unmarried. The doctor, she reports, seems unconcerned about the ethics or legality of such a procedure, and simply said sure, he would do it if she really meant it.

"Continuing her opening statement, she says she would like very much to have a baby. But she does not want to tie herself down to a husband, and she sees no reason why she can not satisfactorily take care of the child. She demonstrates her financial ability, her very good educational background, and she impresses you from the start as being both intelligent and gifted.

"She notes your probable question about some kind of masculine or paternal companionship for the child, and says she sees no problem about supplying that. In effect, however, she says she wants to become a mother without, at least for the present, becoming a wife.

"She needs, nevertheless, she continues, some check from someone like you. If you believe her plan makes sense, at least for her, then she will probably go ahead with it. If, on the other hand, you regard the scheme as indefensible, then she will likely give it up. All this is included in her long opening statement; and from here on, you do what you would actually do if Miss Davis were real and not a role played by Carl Wennerstrom."

MR. CARTWRIGHT: That's very helpful, Miss Davis. You have laid out a general problem. But before I address myself to it with you, I want you to understand something. I'm perfectly willing to give you my best judgment and my best insight—not of course that any one can know the answer to what is essentially *your* problem—but finally you are the one who must make the decision. I'll go along with you, doing with you what I call "fishing," trying to explore with you why this is a problem for you. I may make all sorts of statements, or I may ask all sorts of questions; but I want you to understand from the beginning that such statements and questions will not be intended judgmentally. While we talk, we'll be fishing for understanding with one another in the frame of reference of this particular problem of yours. Is it all right with you if we go ahead on that basis? *You* will finally have to make the decision. I can't decide for you. But now, let's do some fishing. The first thing I want to know is: why do you want a child at all?

MISS DAVIS: Well, I don't see why, as a woman with all the natural hungers and desires including a wish for parenthood, that really has to have much explanation. I think of the creative relationship I would have with the child, how I would share with the child some of the things I have. I'm a professional editor with one of the big magazine chains; did I tell you? I travel a good deal, and I'd like to be able to share some of this excitement and travel with the child.

CARTWRIGHT: Is your father living?

DAVIS: No, he died about four years ago. He was a grand old man. My mother outlived him, and died just last year.

CARTWRIGHT: Are you an only child?

DAVIS: No, I have a sister and two brothers.

CARTWRIGHT: Which one are you?

DAVIS: I'm the youngest. Martha is thirty-seven; I'm thirty-two; and John and Robert are forty-five and forty. Both my brothers are teachers. During the period when my brothers were in school, we all lived near here. Our family was closely knit, actually up to the time I was about twenty-two, when geography and new jobs and things cut down our contacts. We all had very good relationships.

CARTWRIGHT: You had a happy childhood?

DAVIS: Yes, very. I had all the things I wanted and . . . (*trailing off*)

CARTWRIGHT: You're an editor of magazines?

DAVIS: Yes, kind of an editorial troubleshooter, really . . .

CARTWRIGHT: You thought your father loved you just as much as your brothers?

DAVIS: Yes. He was very generous with us girls. He identified more with the boys. He was quite a man himself, masculine appearing, and he had a big, bushy moustache. His friends were like that too; and he liked football, and was concerned that my brothers learn football. But he appreciated the feminine parts of the family too. He wanted us girls to be happily settled in marriage or career, pretty much whatever we wanted to do. (*She pauses.*)

By this time it has become clear to Carl Wennerstrom, and he thought it would have been equally clear to Miss Davis, that Mr. Cartwright, despite his original disclaimers about making decisions, was drawing out all this happy father and happy childhood material in order to pop out eventually with something like: "Do you want your child to be deprived of what meant so much to you?" Further, Mr. Cartwright so far has been trying to get at things in his way rather than Miss Davis'; indeed, his approach looks, in retrospect at least, very rationalistic. So, at this point, Carl Wennerstrom (as Miss Davis) felt that Mr. Cartwright should be shaken a bit. Miss Davis went right along from the pause noted above:

MISS DAVIS (*continuing*): I do have to tell you one thing, Mr. Cartwright. One of my magazines has given me a very important assignment, and I'm leaving very soon to spend six months on the Continent. So I really have to decide pretty soon about the baby, if the doctor can do it in the next few days before I leave. And I'm thirty-two; and if I'm going to do it at all, it should be now. You know fertility decreases from about this age on. I doubt very much that I could find a doctor like this on the Continent; so I would pretty much like to get your view on this within the next hour or so. I'd appreciate it if—

CARTWRIGHT (*partially interrupting*): Did you say you loved your father?

As this question implies, Mr. Cartwright has now explicitly refused to go along with Miss Davis' idea of what he should do. At least so far, he is going to fish in his own way or not at all. There is some more about her brothers, and then:

CARTWRIGHT: You ever been loved?

DAVIS: Sure, sure. I dated a lot, and I went with one fellow for two years, and with another for three years just after college. I have very good relationships with the men on the staff of the magazines. They're very good fellows, and I've known some of them intensely.

CARTWRIGHT: Have you ever had sexual intercourse with men?

DAVIS: Yes.

CARTWRIGHT: With one man for any length of time?

DAVIS: Well, when I was going with this one fellow for two years, we—I guess about the beginning of the second year—both of us felt pretty much the way I feel now, that the social customs and mores were needed, even desperately so; that this was kind of the way in which society kept orderly and coherent; and besides, most people aren't as fortunate as we were on financial resources. I've been extremely lucky on financial investments, and I am, well, more or less independent. So, uh, yes, we began to sleep together; we had an apartment together during that second year. We had a very good relationship, with the full understanding that living together was convenient. It was a terrific experience, and I enjoyed intercourse with him. Then about the end of that second year he was transferred to the Tokyo office and was there for a long time. The second fellow—he was a good friend of the first—well, we didn't set up an apartment; I guess we didn't need to because by that time I had quite an establishment. Anyhow, after a few months I found my sexual relationship to the second fellow even more delightful than it had been to the first. I learned some things about response to him, to his advances, and it was a delightful time.

Perhaps this is a good point for any minister-reader to pause and ask himself how he himself would have responded to these juicy revelations. Otis Rice used to note that ministers, when confronted with a story of this kind, tend to fall into two groups: the "Aha, boy oh boy, tell me more" group, and the "Tut, tut, you know it's wrong" group. Cartwright, however, showed that he was still holding to his original plan.

CARTWRIGHT: Was your father important to you?

In effect, Miss Davis said yes again.

CARTWRIGHT: You say your father was important to you. You say you got a great deal that was very basic that is important to you in your life. And you want to have a child, I understand; but you want to deprive this child of having a father. Is that the way you want to do it?

The cat, which has been whining for some time, is finally let out of the bag, just as Carl Wennerstrom and Miss Davis had guessed. Miss Davis, however, has not exhausted her supply of disconcerting resources.

MISS DAVIS: Oh no, no. As a matter of fact, I don't want to limit my child to just one father. Both Jack and Michael, actually—the two men I lived with as I told you—would make excellent fathers according to all the criteria. But each of them has some limitations; Jack is more aesthetic, and Michael is more athletic. . . . You speak of depriving the child of a father. I look at it quite the other way. I admit I had a very good relationship to my father, but I think that's very rare. I would certainly see that my child was not wholly limited by the qualities of just one person.

CARTWRIGHT: Your brothers, as I recall it, were a good deal older than you?

Cartwright, it continues to be evident, has not been deflected at all from his original path by any of the herrings, red, pickled, or juicy, that Miss Davis has spread in his path. He has shown that he does want to reform something about her or her point of view; and that he is apparently going to stick to his rational collecting of an overwhelming mass of logical data, to which then she will have to give attention, no matter what. But after a few further exchanges about brothers, it becomes evident that Cartwright has had an idea of a different kind:

CARTWRIGHT: Then you had, in your father and your two brothers, three men who were interested in you as a child, who more or less shared your insights. Is that right?

DAVIS: That's right. It was wonderful.

At that point Miss Davis (Wennerstrom) took another look at Cartwright. Even though his rationalism had not cracked an inch, perhaps he was not actually as reformist as he had previously appeared. Or perhaps he was just plain fair, and was willing to look afresh at the contention that a childhood might be happier with three good father figures than with only one. How, then, will Cartwright proceed from here?

CARTWRIGHT: Do you really want a child?
(*He may be back on his original line, or he may not. We must wait and see.*)

DAVIS: Very much. Because I—you know I've had my fling. And I don't want sexual relationships, when they seem good, to stop. But I just wondered if I could, kind of experimentally, try the artificial insemination. I think—maybe—but might it have significance just beyond my experience? You know, there are an awful lot of young widows who've lost their husbands, and . . . (*She trails off.*)

CARTWRIGHT: You're trying to get away with something to see if you can get away with something?

DAVIS: I'm trying to get away with something, yes, but I think it's the way a scientist does with his experiment; where he has a control group and things of that kind, like Kinsey, maybe . . .

CARTWRIGHT: I think Kinsey was fighting society. Are *you* fighting society?

DAVIS: In a way. In a way that a critic of society would fight it.

We may pause at this retrospective point to note that Carl Wennerstrom, in this contribution-to-science and critic-of-society angle, is testing Cartwright's dramatics, as well as some aspects of reformism. On the reformism, he wants to see if the transpersonal (not just for me alone) presentation of the Davis plan will soften Cartwright's suspicion. And on dramatics, provided he can be convincing about the heroine-of-a-new-and-truly-free-world line, he wants to test Cartwright's possible sympathy. But it turns out that Cartwright cannot quite be pigeonholed in either of these ways.

CARTWRIGHT: One of the things which I think may be true —a lot of counseling experience seems to suggest this—is that a strong wish may sometimes be a mask for an opposite wish underneath. We have another notion in the general area of psychiatry which we talk about as ambivalence.

DAVIS: Well, I certainly am ambivalent about this.

CARTWRIGHT: You'll find this kind of condition expressed in Paul where he talks about the fact that what he wants to do he doesn't do and what he doesn't want to do he does. And I don't know, but fishing with you, I'm just wondering whether, for instance, that statement of yours that you want a child, without marriage—that you want to pull this off in society—whether that isn't really just a mask way of your tipping your hat with respect to society? You really don't want a baby—*if* there is truth in this. But I'm just talking and thinking out loud; I don't claim to know. But you say you want an answer in an hour; so—

It now becomes evident that Cartwright has been exploring, all along, the possible situation of Miss Davis in the light of psychodynamic principles deeper than were apparent at the beginning. And that, while continuing to put his speculations about these in I-may-well-be-wrong terms, he is going to articulate them, when it seems they would not throw Miss Davis off her pins, and "test" them out on her. In retrospect we can see that this procedure represents Cartwright's deep convictions about the true nature of dialogue in pastoral care. It is his task (at least his preliminary task) to think out possible ways of accounting for the situation as presented to him, to share his reflections, at what seem the proper points, and to have them tested by the response of the persons to his tentative hunches and hypotheses.

This conception of dialogue, I suggest, is in line with Carl Wennerstrom's concept of distance. If the distance gets too far from either person, it would defeat itself. But if the distance does not eliminate concern and sweating, then it may show a respect which apparently warmer terms like acceptance sometimes take very lightly. It may also, with a touch of rationalism, to be sure, help to establish a "contract" in the relationship, which enables the other person to say what he is prepared to say but protects him from having to say more than that, and which guarantees that the pastor will respond in an honest and structured way to whatever is expressed to him honestly by his parishioner. The actual method demonstrated by Cartwright in the exchanges just reported would have been questioned as much by Carl Wennerstrom, pastoral theologian, as by me. And yet I believe he would have seen beyond this, as I do, to an integrity that transcends the rather abrupt methods. In the realm that is truly basic to effective helping, the minister is now beginning to reveal his great ability, even though, appraised at all other levels, he is under suspicion of "pushing."

After the closeout of the last comment by Cartwright, rather challenging Miss Davis about wanting "an answer in an hour," Wennerstrom's Mephistophelianism again comes to the fore when Miss Davis says:

DAVIS: Oh, I don't want an answer in an hour. I just want your help in reaching a decision.

CARTWRIGHT: Well, I'm trying to dig at insights here much more rapidly than I normally do, in the interest of haste.

She now has him on the run! Presumably, if he followed his normal procedure, he could, within his schedule, engage in almost unlimited fishing expeditions; and since he is smart, by the time he felt it appropriate to reveal his hunches and hypotheses, these could be so logical, so rational, so well supported, that they would at once convince anyone, or at least anyone not in conflict. As it actually is, with the Davis pressure toward soon-or-never, he is short-cutting. It is my retrospective judgment that, at this point, Carl Wennerstrom, even as role-player of Miss Davis, had become a teacher. He had, to put it with great mildness, enormous admiration for Mr. Cartwright. But he still felt that his own special work and insights could, without in the slightest degree violating Cartwright's convictions or tradition, enable him to do a job as good, or better, in less time and with less hoopla about structure.

Just a minute or two after what has been reported there came the following.

CARTWRIGHT: What do you conceive the purpose of sexual intercourse to be?

DAVIS: Well, the furtherance of the race—and pleasure. It feels damn good! And you get to know a person in ways you never can by just talking to him. You can't describe it. (*Here actor Wennerstrom drooled a bit.*)

CARTWRIGHT: I take it, then, that you want to have a child to fulfill yourself.

DAVIS: And the child. I want to share this with the child.

CARTWRIGHT: Want to share what?

DAVIS: Life! Myself! I feel that I've got a lot of contributions to make. I want to fulfill myself, yes. This is a selfish thing so far as it is self-directed. I want to be fulfilled. But I also want this child to be fulfilled.

CARTWRIGHT: Why, specifically, do you prefer test-tube insemination to penis insemination?

DAVIS: Because I know, from what I know of psychoanalysis, that if I were to take Jack for instance . . .

At this point Miss Davis went into a long, cloudy, and highly dubious account about Jack, his good points but his manifest weaknesses, his willingness to father her child but his probably consequent feeling that the child would be his; and she was not sure she would like Jack in the "his" capacity, and so on. After a minute or so of effective recovery from this attempted snow job, Cartwright asked: "Did you like dolls when you were a child?" Miss Davis, being smart, in another minute gets the pitch: "I see what you're getting at. You think I want a child to be a doll, a plaything to play with."

Again she has nailed Cartwright in his tracks. His reply does indeed resort to abstraction; but he does not deny the allegation, seek to define the line his mind was following, or repent of it. He says, "We all have a way of letting our habits carry on to determine our future course . . .

So dolls are disposed of, with the score still about 50–50. Then:

CARTWRIGHT: Are you scared of men?

DAVIS: I'm not scared of men. . . . (*She elaborates.*)

Cartwright then asks her about pleasure in sexual intercourse, and about orgasms. Miss Davis says it's fine, mostly orgasms, and even when not it's still great stuff. Cartwright finally hazards:

CARTWRIGHT: . . . may not be a function of ambivalence between wanting to be a member of the other sex really, and rather resenting your own?

DAVIS: Are you suggesting that I'm a homosexual?

At this point Miss (Wennerstrom) Davis put Mr. Cartwright on the pan for several minutes. In retrospective analysis, this exchange is precisely in keeping with what we have already analyzed; Cartwright is truly sharing his hunches, no matter which way they cut. Just what such sharing might have done to crumble someone who really had unconscious homosexual problems is a matter for appalling conjecture. But whatever Miss Davis' sensitivities, they did not lie at this point. Hence, the very forcefulness, and the distance with which the force was communicated, not only did not impede the relationship, but tended to help it. The almost-worst, so to speak, had been (wrongly) voiced as question: and happily and honestly denied. By all ordinary standards, this was poor counseling. In the actual situation, manifestation of honesty at the very basic level; hence, if "untouchable" areas are not actually involved, rather more pro than con. Would this minister ask something similar of persons genuinely in doubt about being homosexuals? One does not know. If he could stand the responsive trauma, he might still convey honesty and integrity as a cautious rule-follower might not. But the risk is very great.

After getting rid of homosexuality, they returned to the stated problem, and Miss Davis pushed again:

DAVIS: Well, won't you help me make a judgment on this?

CARTWRIGHT: I'll help you in the sense that I'll help you to try to understand yourself with whatever insights about people I've got, sure, and—

DAVIS: But if we just don't move, for instance, wouldn't you vote yes (*meaning: for the artificial-insemination baby*)?

At this point Miss Davis decided to throw Mr. Cartwright back to the interior psychological dynamics, confessed that "I can't trust myself," and elaborated her dubiety, all the time pushing Mr. Cartwright to say yes or no. At first, under this new attack, he analyzed the notion of ambivalence. Miss Davis hit at him by asking if he thought she was "split down the middle"? She then countered by defending her luscious attractions, and all but gave statistics on the offers she had had. Then:

CARTWRIGHT: How many of these men you had no difficulty in attracting were you going to marry, and insist on it?

DAVIS: Insist on it? No. Do you think it was wrong of me to go to bed with Jack and Michael?

CARTWRIGHT: I wasn't there. What do *you* think?
(*Fair! But distant! Miss Davis pays him in his own coin.*)

DAVIS: I'm ambivalent about it.

After ambivalence had been disposed of, Cartwright begins to assume a rather more fatherly approach to the overall situation. Suppose, he asks Miss Davis, had you had, in your childhood, one father one year and another father another year? After some exchange along these lines Miss (Wennerstrom) Davis begins to bring up some taunting, big religious guns: "In your sermon last Sunday you said that God speaks in men and women and continues to speak. In a way I would like to participate in this voice of God, even to thumb my nose at society—yes, in the way that Christ himself did it."

Even Cartwright begins to hide from the big guns. Miss Brave-New-World Davis continues: "I want to create a new relationship—unique—really new. I don't want to fall into a pattern. I don't want to accept a husband, or the necessity of having a husband. Through the gift of God, you might say, a method has become available so that I do not have to be conventional about a husband. I won't even know who the donor is; the doctor will select him. Do you believe that this great new opportunity cannot possibly be the will of God? Why must it be seen as oddball?"

As anyone would, Cartwright made a retreat, but it was strategic. He acknowledged the ambiguities of the world, the inevitablilty of problems even with marriage to the most normal man, the fact that Miss Davis had not found a man she really wanted to marry. Then:

CARTWRIGHT: We can't ever get away from the fact, can we, that we do have to live in society? And that this child is going to have to live in this society. And so I just ask you, as a practical matter, to consider the future of the child, whether because this child is this child or because this child is a part of you.

A bit less nobly, Miss Davis was reminded that school-mates might taunt junior with being a "test-tube child," a regression to a low level of reformism in Cartwright's otherwise ethical discourse. But, nasty gossip out of his system, he concluded with his now accustomed honesty:

CARTWRIGHT: I still don't quite understand what it is or why you feel that you don't want to have this child by a father or a husband.

On such a plaintive note Miss Davis is thrown back on her last resources. She has to admit she likes men, that she is not a promiscuous cat, that a husband might be great stuff, that a husband might be just what she herself needs, if only the personal angle is considered. But she returns (since she must have something still to push) to talk about contribution to society, experimentation in freedom, the legalism of the present-day marriage pattern, and related points. But she is a bit too agile even for the sharp-witted Mr. Cartwright at this point, especially since he is still wholly dedicated to helping *her*. He refuses to be shifted over to helping future generations. But Miss Davis has in effect cut off nearly everything he could think of. For a time he treads water. For instance: "Where are you going to have these affairs, in your apartment where the youngster is going to be, or will you go away?"

Miss Davis, who has her rules of fair play also, does not make the reply about the short distance in feet between where Mr. Cartwright sleeps with his wife, and where their children pound the pillow. She does admit that she believes "yearly fathers" would not be enough. She discusses, no doubt to Mr. Cartwright's envy (since he is only a minister), the role of the governess, tutor, cook, and maid she intends to employ. Mr. Cartwright, by this time, knows he has lost the battle, if not necessarily to Miss Davis, at least to Carl Wennerstrom; so he lets himself go.

CARTWRIGHT: So Johnny gets invited to little Mary's birthday party at the age of nine. Mary's father is there, and he's having a great time. Johnny also gets invited to little Joe's party; also Joe's father is there. So, at Johnny's age nine, what happens? "Johnny, where's your father?" What's he going to answer?

Miss Davis has not lost her wiles. She has already confided to Johnny their contribution to science and human freedom; so woe be unto the conventional child who in the absence of a father declaims bastardhood! Mr. Cartwright is against the wall but not crushed:

CARTWRIGHT: I hope you won't have, twenty years from now, a pantywaist, but I wouldn't bet on it. We live in a world of society whether we like it or not. Your statements suggest that you resent having to come to terms with this society, and with reality generally. You have an illusion that you can change everything. This sounds like some of those dreams you might have had as a little girl, at four or five, hugging your doll and wishing you had a little friend to play with. Now that you have a little money and a little power I wonder if you are not, down underneath, trying to go back there and play—a kind of reliving—with that imaginary child? I am being quite direct because of the time element, when ordinarily I would . . . (*Miss Davis starts to interrupt him.*) I didn't say you have to obey society. From my point of view, you have a right to go and become inseminated and

98

become pregnant and have a child. You do have a right. But if you exercise this right, I'm not sure you are being thoughtful about this new life you will bring into the world. I don't know whether you're being wise about your own future.

Mr. Cartwright then retreats, envisions scarlet fever at six, death in an accident at twelve, and what will Miss Davis do with no husband to comfort her? And he comes back to "these fellows" who will be coming in and out of Miss Davis' bedroom as lacking "depth and lastingness." It seems to hit him hardest that none of them may last.

Ignoring the imputation of casual fornication, Miss Davis pulls the last plug out of her washtub, says she either will or will not get herself inseminated, depending upon what Mr. Cartwright now says in words of one syllable. Despite all the artificial paraphernalia of the role-playing, Mr. Cartwright takes this very seriously, discusses various aspects of the issue with manifest concern and feeling.

CARTWRIGHT: This presents to me a picture of some confusion; and this confusion, it seems to me, in addition to this extraordinary and unusual role you propose for yourself, is an added load. I could wish and pray that if you do this you will have the intelligence and gumption and guts and wisdom and acceptance of yourself so as to make this a good life for yourself and your proposed child. If you are truly able to accept this, I am willing to accept it with you. But I'm not making the decision.

Miss Davis pushes him to a yes or no, then to an "If you were making the decision, would it be yes or no?" Then she taunts him by saying that if she heeds his implication she will say no, and does he approve of that? He concludes, pretty nobly after all:

CARTWRIGHT: If you say you're going to make your decision on the basis of what I know, you're also saying that you have no real basic trust in yourself. How without such basic self-trust and self-respect are you going to get along with the unusual task that you propose for yourself? I refuse to be you. But I do think you need, first, somebody to love, and also somebody who loves you. I've been trying to "love" you in the religious sense; but for your further life, you need the other kind of love, too.

DAVIS: This has been very good. Thank you very much.

P.S. It seems unlikely that she got inseminated.

Long before this role-playing interview with Unitarian Pastor Cartwright, Carl Wennerstrom was a sincere and warm, although not uncritical, admirer of his. He admired Pastor Cartwright on personal qualities, on achievement within the ministry and beyond it to the general community, and on specific instances of courage, compassion, understanding, integrity, and common sense. And yet he would never have applied to Pastor Cartwright, perhaps especially in reference to pastoral care, the word I have used, "model," meaning something to be imitated. Carl Wennerstrom felt that Pastor Cartwright, with all his abilities, even versatility, had dealt too lightly with the emerging knowledge of pastoral care itself; that, indeed, he had used his knowledge of inner psychodynamics to avoid examining critically his own place in pastoral care situations.

However, if Carl Wennerstrom had had to choose between a minister who had all the latest training (even from

Carl Wennerstrom) but could not combine it with the cardinal features of the liberal tradition and Pastor Cartwright, he would undoubtedly have chosen the latter.

If my own running appraisal of Pastor Cartwright is, as I trust it is, a reasonable facsimile of what Carl Wennerstrom would have said, then even I (as some kind of non-Unitarian liberal) am impressed by Pastor Cartwright; his integrity, his honesty, his sticking-by-his-principles, even his honest admissions of being disconcerted, and by the strength as well as the weakness in his adherence to the paradoxical characteristics identified by Carl Wennerstrom.

I have a sneaking suspicion that Pastor Cartwright is afraid that paying serious attention to writings like my own might tempt him to qualify or compromise his pastoral integrity. Even he would concede, I think, that such attention would help him in certain tight places. But he is the kind of liberal who "truly lives" in tight places, and on deserts, and is not at all sure that he wants any kind of help from Presbyterian cases at such points.

From my actual point of view, I admire his independence as well as his integrity. On one point I can reassure him: I would not substitute any amount of technique, method, or know-how for his integrity. If he feels threatened by them, that is, almost to quote him, his problem and not mine. On the other point, involving his desert-well-digging equipment, I rather suspect that Pastor Cartwright and I may have a parting of the ways. I think, with all his virtues, he dug some unnecessary wells—the homosexual one, for instance. I hope he will keep his spirit. But I hope he will not be threatened when some of our water wagons pass by.

I believe Carl Wennerstrom would have said: here is a minister who represents in very great measure and with unique virtues of his own the very best in the liberal tradition; but here, too, is a minister who can be even better than he now is if he corrects any possible one-sided interpretations of rationalism, reformism, dramatics, and distance that he now has. But even as he is now, the liberal tradition need apologize to no one.

RESPONSE AND REBUTTAL

Anonymous

As the minister known here by the pseudonym of "Mr. Cartwright," I was invited to comment especially on the preceding chapter but also upon all the previous chapters of this book. I shall do so under three headings: first, an appreciation of Carl Wennerstrom's thesis and of his specialized ministry; second, some general remarks on counseling; and finally, comments on Seward Hiltner's analysis of Mr. Cartwright as "a (partial) model" for pastoral care.

An Appreciation

Carl Wennerstrom chose for himself a specialized hospital ministry, which was also a teaching ministry in an exploratory sense. In his ministry, concern for pastoral counseling, which in the parish ministry is necessarily one of several major ministerial functions, was for him paramount. Accordingly, parish ministers may tend to write off Wennerstrom's specialized dedication and his thesis in this book as that of an enthusiast and specialist and so "not for us."

It is doubtful whether

103

thoughtful ministers will be able to defend themselves from the Wennerstrom thesis by so simple
an argument. Wennerstrom may overload his notion of
a paradox "which borders on contradiction." The fact remains that his analytical use of the categories of rationalism,
reformism, dramatics, and distance as instruments for better
understanding and self-understanding of liberals in and out
of the religious institution is in itself an almost irresistibly
intriguing device. It may be the reasonable, reformative,
dramatic, and cool way of bringing the liberal's paradoxical
stance into therapy if not under judgment. Hopefully, it
may bring us more fully to ourselves and into more significant communication with one another.

On Counseling

It was not in the context of a rationalistic-enlightenment
utopianism that Cartwright (I) developed his first dedications to the ministry. It was rather in the context of a
creedal, otherworldly utopian promise that seemed to fail
people in this world.

Teen-age reaction to a ministry of that point of view
whose blindness, unconcern, or callousness in regard to the
quality of particular persons' lives in a specific situation in
his parish and community generated in him the rather angry
decision "to be a minister" and "a better minister than that."
As means to that end the teen-age Cartwright developed
this simple theory of the ministry which included teaching,
preaching, and counseling: "Get to know all kinds of people in all kinds of situations well enough so that you can
help them when they need it."

When he first formulated that intentional statement for
himself, Cartwright believed, rationalistically, that it was

possible to get to know people and situations in the world as well as he knew the multiplication tables, in which case "answers" to human need would become as available as the answer to eight times nine. Naïve, of course. He did dramatize himself as the prime agent of reformative help. He did suppose that when people needed help they knew it, and would seek it (often from him in the study or in the pulpit or on the street!), and that they would be eager to improve not only their environment but also themselves.

This was determinedly optimistic. He thought the cross he heard about on Sundays was chiefly a symbol of the injustice some people suffer at the hands of others. That's what he heard of what he was told. He did not know that it might also symbolize the fact that when we are serving the best causes, the worst can happen to them and to us; that sometimes, wanting to do our best, we are at our worst; that sometimes when help to persons or in a situation is most needed, everyone involved is or seems to be incapable of helping; that "trying anything" may be worse than doing nothing; and that showing too much concern may be as bad as not having any.

There is one thing about Cartwright which he has sometimes thought a grace and sometimes a curse; he has always cared for "all sorts and conditions" of people, nearby and far away, especially those in trouble. He never could divorce himself from those he loved. It is the second phrase of T. S. Eliot's wise admonition, "to care and not to care," that he finds very hard to come by even as he affirms it as wisdom for would-be counselors. To care without insisting, holding, moulding, etc. To honor selfhood in one's own self and in other selves is easy when interests and goals are concurrent; but not easy when differences are polarized, crippling, or killing.

105

To care and not to care. To be ready to try to help or willing not to try to help. To welcome interdependent relationships; to refuse the gifts or the demands of the abjectly dependent, favoring rather their hopefully developing integrity. Cartwright never needed to be told to care. He needed to learn even to impose on himself the rule of "uncaring." To care mightily how it all comes out in any situation—and not to care. I am my brother's helper—maybe.

Even when I'm sure about "help" one way or another, I cannot be sure. Satisfaction in counseling comes chiefly out of trying one's best with the other or others. Success and failure are secondary considerations. Both are finally for history and God to decide. For Cartwright: to care and not to care, sometimes both demands indicated in a single moment. So much for attitude in counseling.

As to method: Cartwright knew more surely about it when he was younger and believed that one could really find the whole truth and convey it systematically.

In reaction to literalistic and idolatrous interpretations of Christian theology, he was once very sure that theology was so much eyewash. Freud's notions he once thought scientific truth rather than the mythology which Freud once told Einstein they were. Adler once "had it" from Cartwright's point of view; then Jung; then Reik; then the Gestaltists. The semanticists seemed to have it for a period; then Northrop and the epistemologists, and so on.

All have it, and nobody has it, really. The human thinking process is complex beyond full charting or systematization. Our theories are mythological structures. As more than one recent psychologist has asserted, many systems work more or less as counseling aids. Or perhaps it is not any systematically stated method that works, but Holy Spirit, Creative Unconscious, Interpersonality, the Continuing Creator,

X. Counseling may be a good thing. Something good may happen in it that would not otherwise take place. Growth may proceed more rapidly through counseling than without it.

Counseling may also be a bad thing. At least for months or years counselors may be turned into tin gods, and counselees be confirmed in their wormhood. Cartwright may be a good, bad, or indifferent counselor at any sitting. Rereading Reich or Hiltner before each session might make it better, or worse.

Hiltner seems to think he knows; but he too is caught in our fallible human predicament. Cartwright is presented as "a (partial) model for liberal pastoral care"—remember. In the good old days a model person was considered the ideal incarnate. Now scientists use the term model to indicate that they know their more-or-less systematized findings are partial, not the final reality. Like most of us, Hiltner will not give up searching for model realizations of the ideal. Like many of us, the best he can find is a (partial) model. A working model of a man, minister, and sometime counselor (that works more or less well) is the way Cartwright would think of himself; and this despite all his persisting attempts to improve himself and his methods. Through all such efforts he has been fishing around for self-understanding, for understanding of other people in the study, for understanding of other counselors and their theories of divers sorts, and finally for theological understanding.

So, Cartwright: take all you know and do not know—take experience, trial and error, faith, caring and not caring—into the study and "fish" with another person or persons for understanding of them and for their understanding of your understanding. Explore the fishing grounds, of course.

Try to locate significant pools to search in. Do this very consciously; but then lose yourself in the casting about in those pools. See if the other person too may get lost in them and in being lost, just possibly be re-created.

Through the years Cartwright as counselor has found the courage to "trust his unconscious" more and more for guidance. Or, with different theological flavor, call it Holy Spirit at work in the situation. Calling it X or Y is not so important as learning to trust the process itself, and all the grace that may be engendered in it.

Sometimes conscious and unconscious reasonings will be in long debate in the counselor, for minutes or for days: about what to ask, what to say, how to say it, or what not to say or do. The one tests the other. In the first years of counseling I would not trust myself (unconscious) very much. After all, I was reading and mixing with the experts for the first time. Therefore reason (conscious) used theories in handlike maps of the pond and set out to see how the territory it fished in fitted the map. Not so much any more. Yes, there are many maps of the pond we fish in for understanding. But maps are for traveling, and traveling proves all maps incomplete at best, and at worst, but some other traveler's bad hunch. Not only one's own but other people's "inspiration" may be demonic. Trust Spirit, and unconscious minding process, but never without at least a little rational query. Fish. Try. Get understanding or generate it if you can. Insight and healing may have come last week (while one was not looking), and are now, surprisingly, only to be celebrated. It may happen today; ten years from now; or never.

Care. Think. Fish for understanding. Be open to inspiration. Test it. Study. Trust the process. Take some chances but don't rush anything. Fish, rather than rush or be rushed.

Keep heart and mind and spirit and study door open for another possible try another day.

To himself Cartwright as counselor has sometimes seemed more stupid and inept than even he could imagine himself to have been; sometimes wiser and more helpful than he would ever have believed; sometimes as if he and "the minister's study" were but instruments of the devil, or of God's grace. Perhaps the strangest fact of all is that sometimes what felt at the time like "grace abounding" was later discovered to be a very mixed blessing; while what was "the very devil" in the short run sometimes turned out to be a seeming revelation of the dark side of the face of God the Creator.

According to the ancient Mosaic revelation of faith, there is said to be in the givenness of life both good and evil, a blessing and a curse. If in the holy givenness of that revelation, goodness and blessing are to be found, it will therefore necessarily be in the midst of the good in association with the apparent cursed evil. It happens that way; perhaps it may be helped to happen. No minister in or out of the study has a right to suppose that it *must* happen that way. No minister worthy of the name will give up on the probability that it is possible for us to find in life, despite all its hells, blessedness and happiness, or that they may find us.

It strikes me that Carl Wennerstrom's four principal categories may be very relevant as applied to counseling itself.

First, use *reason* for all it is worth; but faith in the process or in God's holiness is more trustworthy, being inclusive of reason and of much else, too.

Second, *reform* if you can and be open to being reformed;

but ethical reform is never as radical as reform of being in the direction of religious insights.

Third, we are "in being" in a life-and-death *drama* which presents itself variously as tragedy, comedy, farce, etc. Dramatic role-playing and roles are no substitute for religious living even when artily contrived; but all life is dramatic.

Fourth, essentially "all that is, is of a piece." We are all "members one of another," or "children of God," whether we like it or not. All that is, is interrelated. In the end, however alone we may come to feel, we are cursed or blest, we live and we die, together. To keep that *distance* from others which, as much as may be, keeps us off their necks and them off ours, is important to do; but we, friends or enemies, are in the same boat, and cannot escape sharing lives and lot. God our Creator and our Judge simply will not have it so in the givenness of things.

Comments on Commentary

Presented with the first chapters of this volume, Cartwright's first response was appreciation that the editors should undertake such a labor of love in Carl Wennerstrom's memory. That appreciation persists. The chapters then brought to recollection the "game of counseling" that Wennerstrom for his own studiously serious purposes wanted to play with Cartwright. By now that game may be interesting to the reader in various ways: what it says about Wennerstrom, about the imaginary Miss Davis, about the anonymous Cartwright, about Hiltner, and finally about counseling.

As Wennerstrom and Cartwright first sat down to the counseling game, Cartwright had first of all to decide whether he would be more interested in Wennerstrom or in his projected imaginary counselee, who turned out to be Miss Davis. Willfully he decided to "play it straight," to take Wennerstrom's Miss Davis as nearly for real as he could. Despite this effort there were several times in his hour with Miss Davis when it became apparent that Wennerstrom rather than she was responding to Cartwright, with his own hidden purposes and considerable expertise in counseling.

In such instances Wennerstrom understood something about the pool in which Cartwright was fishing for understanding, and was obviously pressing Cartwright, or wanting him to change the subject. Editor Hiltner also sensed these roadblocks or switches and apparently delighted in them as if the Wennerstrom game were simply a contest, which counseling may sometimes indeed become when hunches are being seriously tested. Cartwright believes that even the most serious counseling, like all fishing, should have its fun side and its contests; but contest-in-counseling may easily become too pervasive to be good counseling.

If it appears that Wennerstrom, Hiltner, and Cartwright belong to a little mutual admiration society, Cartwright would however express one disappointment with Hiltner's otherwise perceptive comments. That is that Hiltner's own theological grounding is scarcely mentioned except in an acid comment or two injected at the end of the commentary, and then only in a most generalized way. It is apparent he feels that Cartwright, as a liberal, "is not at all sure that he wants any kind of help from Presbyterian cases at such points!" It is not any kind of help from any kind of source, from Moses to Hiltner, that Cartwright seeks to avoid. He has studied as widely and as deeply as his ministerial life allows. Yet for all their real or possible insights and understandings, Cartwright takes all counseling *systems* with a grain of salt. He believes from much experience that not knowing the answers is no more dangerous than, as Josh Billings said, "knowing so much that isn't so." Systems may easily become Procrustean beds that mutilate more than they free the spirit.

Where is the theological breadth and depth in Hiltner? Cartwright is convinced that most of the difficulties that bring people to counselors are basically the result of a religious faith and theology which are either lacking or faulty. Telling Cartwright that he shies away from "Presbyterian cases" is shoddy counseling. What cases, at what points? Actually, among other things Cartwright is in his own understanding of the doctrine a little bit of a predestinarian! Intellectually, he is not sure, but emotionally he feels that way in some situations. Yet as a minister he has no right to give up on anybody.

It seems to Cartwright that what brought Miss Davis to the study was a faulty enlightenment theology which, up to a point, had worked for her. Indeed, it was tempting her to play the role of God with the life of a possible child. Oh, a loving God she would be—but would she? Did she have the courage and wisdom even to try it, let along bring it off? If she had had clearly either the courage or the compulsion to do so, she would never have visited Cartwright; would she?

That much seemed clear in Wennerstrom's first introduction of Miss Davis. Why did Miss Davis want to play (father and mother) God? Why did she not have the courage (or the compulsion) to do so? Why did a stranger, whom she had once heard preach, seem so much an authority that she would trust the life of a child in her womb to his decision? Miss Davis was not ready even to understand most of these questions as such. Cartwright did not get

112

answers to most of them. He did not ask Miss Davis most of them. Cartwright must admit that his questions may not have been the best questions to try to ask or to explore. Still, there she was, asking a question that was not really the question, and seeking an answer that would not really answer.

What Cartwright tried to do was to show her that he cared for her (and that possible child), and to let her know in one way or another that he would be available in his study should she ever come that way again to get on with other and perhaps deeper questions. Since she, whatever her problems, did not appear to be psychotic, one thing Cartwright would not do was to assume her responsibility for her. In that regard, although he cared, he knew that he should neither care nor really decide, *for her.*

MENTAL HEALTH AND PASTORAL CARE IN THE LIBERAL CHURCHES

Harry C. Meserve

Carl Wennerstrom's striking chapter on ministers' attitudes toward pastoral care underlines some of the special problems of the liberal church which are ever present but too often not faced or even recognized.

The liberal church is a very special kind of religious institution. One might even say that logically and intellectually it should not exist at all. How can there be a church which is a fellowship of shared belief, commitment, and purpose when these things do not exist in any way that can be clearly defined to the satisfaction of all concerned? There is no creed, no commonly accepted form of worship, no sacrament, no basic commitment—except the commitment to freedom itself—that unites the liberal church. Yet the liberal church does undeniably exist. It has maintained a continuous existence in America for nearly a hundred fifty years. From very small beginnings it has shown a rate of growth that compares favorably with that of most other churches. It has an active and educated clergy, has played an honorable part in the social and

114

political and religious development of American life, and fills the role for the people who belong to it of a genuine spiritual home.

The liberal minister, like other ministers, priests, and rabbis, conducts services of worship, preaches sermons, directs a program of religious education, performs weddings, funerals, and christenings (usually called dedications), participates in community leadership, and of course in the process of his work counsels with his people about their personal problems.

No statistics that I know of are available to show whether the average liberal minister does more or less personal counseling than his colleagues in the other churches. I suspect that this is an individual matter determined by the answers to such questions as: How available is the minister for personal counseling? How vigorously does he stress this aspect of his ministry? How much training and experience has he had? Is his personality the kind that inspires confidence and trust? These questions, and in particular the last one, are probably more decisive than his theology in determining the counseling activity of any minister. My own experience, for what it may be worth, is that once a minister becomes established in his church and personally known to the members of his congregation, he will have as much counseling as he is able to take care of, and probably more. This assumes that he will not undertake long-range counseling and psychotherapy, but will refer people who need this kind of help to responsible professionals.

The Problems of the Liberal Minister

Wennerstrom is, in my view, quite right in his analysis of some of the special problems and attitudes a liberal minister finds in the task of counseling. Lacking a commonly accepted theological framework, he is tempted to take too much responsibility and to think of himself as an "answer man" who is failing if he cannot come up with specific solutions to the various problems that are brought before him. As one who tends to seek rational and ideal solutions, he is often disturbed by the large element of irrationality and tragedy in human predicaments and behavior. There is much that he cannot explain or account for. So many things happen that in a rational scheme of things ought not to happen. The presence of sin and tragedy in the midst of life is a brute fact for which he has no answers in his philosophy. Seldom if ever can he say "God understands this, even if we do not: we must therefore trust in his goodness and mercy."

Nor can he have recourse to such aids as prayer and Bible reading and the ritual acts which have real healing effects among orthodox believers. Often, as a liberal minister, I have wished that the liberal church did provide such words and acts which have the effect of symbolizing each individual's relationship to the continuing faith and visible community of the church. But the liberal minister is without these aids when he confronts his healing task.

Furthermore, I do not doubt that the liberal minister may suffer from the feeling of social distance which Wennerstrom describes so vividly. He would probably prefer to map out a therapeutic program for the one who comes to him for help rather than to take on the more sensitive and exacting task of going down into the depths with the sufferer and meeting his despair with him. It is always easier to say "This or that you ought to do" than to enter personally into the perplexity and discouragement of another and counsel with him as he seeks to find a way through.

116

The Strengths of the Liberal Minister

But with all these admittedly serious handicaps, the liberal minister does have some strengths in the counseling task. After all, he is a man; and if he is a man who genuinely cares about others, his caring and concern are his greatest assets in the counseling process. If he cannot offer the love of God, he can offer the disinterested love of another human being and a willingness to listen and to understand.

Again, while he cannot offer explanations for, he can offer acceptance of, the sadness and tragedy that are an inevitable part of the human condition. After all, there is no healing possible beyond the most superficial levels unless and until men are able to accept themselves as finite human beings and the world around them as full of incompleteness and uncertainty in which approximations but not ultimate fulfillments of our values and aims are the best we can hope for. Perhaps in such a world as this the grace of acceptance is a more practical and helpful gift than is reassurance that everything will somehow come out all right in the end. We must face the fact that everything may not come out all right in the end; but that, even so, life is worth living and some good thing can be attained.

The liberal minister, like any other minister, also has behind him the support of the church as a caring community. People in a liberal church are anxious to be helpful to one another in time of need, and the minister brings to his pastoral task a communal goodwill and sympathy that can have very practical results for those in trouble. All that is needed is a suggestion by him, and this helping power is released for the benefit of those with whom he counsels. One of the heartening discoveries that the liberal minister makes—and it is no less true of other churches—is that his

117

congregation contains numerous individuals with special skills in a number of different areas who are only waiting to be called upon to help in the therapeutic task of the church. The minister must, of course, use discretion and careful judgment in the way in which he calls upon these skills in specific instances, but the presence of the religious community and its desire to help are perhaps the most powerful therapeutic resources that any minister has available to him.

It is an interesting paradox that in a church that denies theological and ecclesiastical authority the minister does all the same have considerable authority in his own right. This authority differs from the authority of the clergyman in many denominations in that it does not rest upon the mere fact of his vocation and ordination. In the liberal church the minister, although he is professionally trained and ordained as a clergyman, wins such authority as he possesses through the process of exerting democratic leadership. First of all, he has been chosen by the people of his church—probably an overwhelming majority of them—to be their religious leader and spokesman. Once so chosen, however, it remains for him to earn and win his leadership role by his sincerity, his understanding of his people's needs and problems, and by the trust which he can inspire as one who is genuinely and disinterestedly concerned for the welfare of the church and of each individual in it. Once this kind of authority has been established, and as long as it is responsibly and sensitively used, there is no other authority to compare with it. The minister who has earned it can exert a very wide freedom of judgment and action. People will listen to what he says and accept from him difficult truths which they would accept from nobody else except, perhaps, the family physician. This authority has no legal or supernatural sanctions. It is the result of what Martin Buber would have called a genuine I-Thou relation between the minister and his people. It should be noted too that if a clergyman of any denomination fails to earn this kind of leadership and authority in his church, external legal or supernatural sanctions will prove of no avail. The health of a church as a religious community and hence its effectiveness as a therapeutic community rest in the end upon this delicate relationship between minister and congregation. It is fragile in many ways, and can be quickly lost through the blindness or impetuousness of a minister or the misunderstanding or mistaken zeal of members of a congregation. It must be carefully nourished by both minister and congregation through the changing weathers of a church's life and growth. When this relationship is sound and healthy it is one of the deepest and strongest of all human relationships, and its healing power for those who avail themselves of it is incalculable.

It is for this reason that there is a real difference between religious counseling—by which I mean counseling within the context of this minister–church-member relationship—and the kind of counseling which is based on a one-to-one relationship between a professionally trained counselor and his client or patient. Without in any way denigrating the second relationship and, indeed, with full recognition of its appropriateness and effectiveness in many areas of human need, I think it is possible to say that the minister–church-member relationship contains unique dimensions. It is both personal and communal. It presupposes and uses a common ground in the shared life of the religious community. It includes the basic values, hopes, and faith which the religious community has made its own. It incorporates what Gordon Allport has called the intrinsic religion of those involved.

This kind of relationship has therapeutic possibilities that are not found in the more strictly professional relationship. The presence of this added dimension is as real in the liberal church as in any other church. Often it is not clearly recognized, but whether recognized and defined or not it provides the liberal minister with a genuine pastoral role and with the essential human resources to carry it on.

The Liberal Church Congregation

Turning from the liberal minister to the people with whom he works in his church, there are, I think, several distinctive characteristics of the members of liberal churches which apply in a majority of cases. A large percentage—well over 60 percent of the people in liberal churches today—were not born and brought up in the liberal church. They come to it out of some other church and denomination or out of the large unchurched segment of our population. In the case of those who come from other more orthodox churches and denominations the persons involved probably went through a crisis of belief during which they rejected the religious doctrines and practices of their childhood. After that, in many cases, they went through a period during which they rejected all churches and all, or almost all, religious beliefs, only to come at length, often through marriage and parenthood, to the felt need for a religious community, if not a theological world view.

The other group, those who come from nonchurch and nonreligious backgrounds, arrive in the liberal church with the same need for a religious community in which they and their children can play a part but with a built-in suspicion of all religious beliefs and of the religious institution itself.

I call this attitude the "rebellion syndrome." In the case

120

of those who have come out of one of the orthodox churches it includes rejection of beliefs and practices that were in the former religious situation and of anything in the new situation that is reminiscent or even comparable to the old. There is a strong impulse to move entirely out of the Christian background and to create an entirely new religion made up of entirely non-Christian elements. In twentieth-century America this is very hard to do because our culture, although highly secular, is rooted in the Judeo-Christian tradition, and its moral and spiritual language, its symbolism, its rituals, and even its profanity belong to that tradition.

A typical example of this anti-Christian impulse was provided in a group of Unitarians who were discussing how to interpret Christmas to their children. The Babylonian recognition of the winter solstice was found acceptable. The feast of Bacchus and the Roman Saturnalia were seen as important elements in the Christmas season, as were also Hanukkah, Santa Claus, and certain Druidical symbols like the pine boughs and the mistletoe. When the minister shyly suggested that there was also a long-standing connection between Christmas and the celebration of the birth of Jesus, this was scornfully dismissed as mythological and orthodox.

A second characteristic of the rebellion syndrome is the rejection of words and practices connected with the former religious tradition. In many liberal churches one does not pray, one meditates; one does not worship, one celebrates; one does not listen to a sermon, but to an address; one does not sing hymns, but songs; one does not celebrate Easter, but springtime; one is not christened, but dedicated.

The unfortunate thing about this effort to break with the immediate past is that too often the rebels impoverish their own lives by rejecting not only the words and practices of their former religious tradition, but also the things for which they stand as well. Religious beliefs, rituals, and symbols are related to deep and universal experiences of human life. The rebels find themselves still having these experiences. Their emotional hungers and needs continue, but they are cut off from the old framework of meaning and have no new one within which they can accept, understand, and live through these experiences.

A third aspect of the rebellion syndrome is a kind of noisy self-assertion, a *hubris*, that arises out of the excitement and stimulation of the newly found freedom. Freedom is a heady experience. To move out of authoritarianism in religion and to assert one's own individuality by denying God, the supernatural, sin, and the need for forgiveness and redemption without incurring any divine wrath or punishment gives many people for a while a great sense of emancipation and self-sufficiency. It is only later that they realize that the persistent perplexities of human life continue, and must be met with something more than mere denial of the old answers and the assertion of freedom. This *hubris* involves a kind of brittle intellectualism, an attitude that seems to say "If I cannot understand it, it cannot be so." It is difficult for the minister to deal with this attitude, not only because it leaves no room for wonder or reverence, but also because it leaves no room for self-examination and that openness toward life's as-yet-undiscovered possibilities which is the key to human growth and development. The first essential of successful therapy is a sense of need, and those caught in the rebellion syndrome cannot admit that sense of need.

The rebellion syndrome as it appears in those who come into the liberal church from a nonreligious background is less acute. They have not so much to reject and are better able to accept the liberal point of view for what it is: a search for values and meanings in an ever-changing world. Their major problem is a fear of commitment which they share with those emerging from other churches. This fear of commitment is based upon a misunderstanding of freedom in its religious dimension. Freedom does not mean lack of conviction. It means the right to choose, and to use the mind freely in choosing, the convictions by which we shall live. It also implies the changing of conviction as new knowledge and new experience show the way. It is easy to understand why the rebellion syndrome includes fear of commitment. Those who have broken their ties with an orthodox church look back on its demands for personal commitment as an imprisonment of the mind and a denial of freedom which they do not want to experience again. Those who have hitherto looked at religion from the outside see the church and its commitments as a possible threat to the freedom they have enjoyed. They are wary of responsibilities that may prove burdensome or limiting. "I enjoy coming to the church, hearing the talks, and taking part in the discussions," remarked an intelligent and highly articulate young man, "but I do not want to join the church. It might limit my freedom of thought and action." This is a common attitude in the liberal church. It reveals a frequent confusion of freedom with lack of responsibility.

The rebellion syndrome in the liberal church has a duration in most cases of from two to three years, after which those who have experienced it enter into a more rational and responsible attitude toward the church itself and their own personal search for meaningful values and goals. The liberal minister must be aware of the existence and power of the syndrome if his counseling is to be effective. People

123

involved in this process have the same problems and needs as other people.

The concept of social distance applies not only to the liberal minister but also to many of the people in the liberal church. Emotional involvement both in a religious and social sense often seems an admission of weakness, and hence people are reluctant to turn to their minister for help in time of stress or perplexity. The liberal minister, if he has understood and mastered his own diffidence when it comes to dealing with people at deep emotional levels, will know how to bridge this distance with his people. It is a skill that requires considerable patience, persistence, and, above all, sincerity and genuine concern.

In spite of these attitudes, the people in a liberal church are genuinely interested in religion and are eager to talk about it. Since religious beliefs are no longer in a special category where doubt and questioning are forbidden, they can be discussed freely in the same way that anything else can be discussed. In general, people are more ready to discuss religious questions than their own personal problems and perplexities. They tend to be more reticent about their personal difficulties, and when they are led by severe pressures to discuss their problems with their minister they are apt to apologize about doing so: "I hate to bother you with this," or "I ought to be able to handle this myself but . . ."

Ministering to the Liberal's Unique Problem

This brings us to the heart of the liberal's problem. He has abandoned faith in a supernatural god and in the various symbolic and mystical dimensions of religion. He believes, or professes to believe, in a rational and naturalistic view of life. Therefore it should be possible for him as a free, rational being to put his own life in order, making and carrying through the necessary conscious decisions that are required to solve his problems. At the same time he is a human being who lives not only at the conscious, rational level but at the unconscious, emotional level as well. But if he accepts this fact he fears that he will lose his liberalism and become enmeshed for the first time or again, as the case may be, in a sentimental, emotional, supernatural view of life that will make it impossible for him to think clearly and freely.

The liberal minister's task is often that of helping his people to accept the emotional-instinctive part of their human nature and to realize that in so doing they need not sacrifice reason and their liberal faith. A purely rational religion is inevitably an incomplete religion, since so much of life is lived at the unconscious level and so many of our decisions have emotional as well as rational sources and overtones. Once this more complete and realistic view of human nature and behavior has been accepted and incorporated into liberal religious thought, it will make room for the attitudes of warmth and feeling which are often so sadly lacking in the worship and group life of the liberal churches.

It will also make room for commitment, not to the dogmatic beliefs of the past, but to the living and unfolding purposes of religion in the world today. Far from being a limiting and confining experience, genuine commitment is a liberating and exhilarating experience. It sets one free from the aimless and the trivial and from the frustration and boredom of the merely novel. The temptation to become a religious dilettante is a great one in the liberal church and must be resisted, since mere freedom is not sufficient ground for a healthy religion.

The task of the liberal minister as counselor and guide is to help his people become part of a continuing quest, a journey toward self-discovery and toward heightened usefulness in the world. He cannot offer them safety in this world or salvation in the next. He can offer the support and strength that come with giving themselves to the service of creative ethical values in this world. This is not an easy matter, and the liberal minister too often finds himself offering one good cause after another when what his people need is the kind of caring and understanding that enable them to be more completely human in the situations where they actually are. Wennerstrom's figure of the hypothetical Unitarian on the day of the crucifixion running downtown to see if he can get a stay of execution from Pilate is too true to be comfortable.

Yet I believe there is a rising awareness among Unitarian and other liberal ministers of the need for a faith and an approach to human problems that offer something more than social or political involvement and education. This awareness is evident both in the growing number of seminary students who see clinical-pastoral training as an important part of their preparation for the ministry, and in the numerous ministers I have talked with who feel a real desire to make the counseling aspects of their ministry more effective.

The liberal churches today are made up for the most part of highly educated people who belong to the privileged section of our population. There are probably fewer than there once were of the very rich, but there are hardly any of the very poor. They regard the church not so much as a haven of comfort and safety, but rather as a community of freedom within which each can carry on his search for life's meaning. The minister's task is to provoke thought and the spirit of discovery rather than to provide answers.

126

His entire task is a counseling task at both its public and private levels if we accept Curran's definition of counseling: "to help people take counsel with themselves." The minister's preaching, his educational leadership, his community work, as well as his personal counseling, need to have a sensitive therapeutic dimension. This does not mean he must abandon his prophetic role. It does mean that he must study carefully how ideas are communicated and how acceptance and understanding of them are won.

I have recently had the interesting and stimulating experience of returning to the full-time parish ministry of a liberal church after some seven years. Several strong impressions have come to me about the liberal church as a religious community.

The first impression concerns the tremendous religious hunger that exists among religious liberals. These people are not running away from religion but reaching out for it. Their denials, the rebellion syndrome, are merely the negative side of a profound desire for religious experience and religious affirmation in terms that they can accept intellectually and apply to their own lives in the world. This hunger is not fed by preaching, however eloquent and well-informed. It is satisfied better by the exchange of ideas and feelings within the context of small groups. What is needed and sought is the feeling of companionship in the search for faith sufficient unto the day and confidence that tomorrow will provide tomorrow's sufficiency. The liberal church offers a way of living in the midst of uncertainty and perplexity, not the removal of these conditions of human existence.

The second impression has to do with the depth and intensity of the feelings and concerns that exist among the people of the liberal church. Where formal and traditional answers are left behind them, the problems them-selves stand out with heightened clarity. In trying to help his people the liberal minister cannot get away with a formal prayer or a verse of scripture. He must, if he is to be useful at all, bridge the social distance and go with them into the real experiences they are having, preserving at the same time the professional detachment necessary to his own sta-bility. He must learn, in Eliot's phrase "to care and not to care." Hence he must maintain his own mental health and stability.

My third impression relates to the dignity and the diffi-culty of the minister's task. "It is," says a friend of mine, a minister, "a great compliment and responsibility when a group of people ask a man to talk with them and share with them the most important experiences of life." It is easy to forget this fact in the press of everyday life. It is easy for a minister to take as a matter of course what is a profoundly moving experience for one of his people. Hence it is essential for him to keep his heart open and sensitive while guarding himself at the same time against overinvolvement, a hard but not impossible task, as every professional man knows.

To sum up, the cure of souls is as vital a part of the liberal church as it is of any other church. The absence of a fixed theological framework presents some problems but also offers some challenges and opportunities. The liberal minister is, in my experience at least, increasingly aware of the importance of this aspect of his ministry. The liberal churches welcome, appreciate, and use all the skills and all the caring the minister is able to bring.

THE
DOCTRINE
OF MAN
IN LIBERAL
THEOLOGY

John F. Hayward

It is an honor to contribute an essay in liberal theology to the memory of a man whose life so fully expressed the spirit of religious liberalism. Carl Wennerstrom was a man of action and robust courage. He was also a patient and sympathetic man, undismayed by weakness and able to dwell in quietness among the poor in spirit. He honored his fellow Unitarians for their courageous activism. But when he came to contemplate their one-sided religious witness with its activistic bias he was also moved to engage in the study and the writing of which the present volume bears the fruit. In a religion oriented to talent and success, he took up the cause of human defeat.

The Image of the Hero

Midway through his first chapter Wennerstrom throws out an intriguing speculation: "I have sometimes wondered, incidentally, if this dramatic penchant for trailblazing, and this boredom with any partially established trail, may not put the liberal *en rapport* with the hero myths of so many cultures, in which the hero always, despite his trials and tribulations, finally slays the dragon and gets the girl; as against, for example, the New Testament parable of the prodigal son, where the son's trail-blazing effort was a fiasco and his self-identity was restored only by his father's forgiveness."

This suggestion of the heroic presuppositions of the liberal's religion is well taken. Granted that the modern hero is more cerebral and less athletic than his classical prototypes, the common element is a certain courage of self-dependence and a desire to take action in every situation no matter how difficult. In the dark days of 1938, Frederick M. Eliot, then President of the American Unitarian Association, wrote of Unitarianism:

It is not a faith for those who have surrendered to fatigue, or yielded to the insidious arguments of the old men who no longer dream dreams. It is a sober optimism, because the plain facts of the world's condition today leave no place for jaunty or careless optimism; but it *is* optimism, and it is not ashamed to be called by that name.[1]

Eliot's reliance upon the spirit of youth is an important tie to the heroic spirit. As ancient Greek literature and sculpture glorified the young, showing immortally youthful gods and celebrating heroes who often died in youth, so the heroism of modern religious liberalism consciously and unconsciously focuses upon the virtues of young men or men young in spirit. The destiny of human well-being is vested essentially in youthful strength including that found in those who even in old age retain a youthful outlook.

[1] Frederick May Eliot, *Unitarians Believe* (Boston: American Unitarian Association, 1940), p. 26.

In the essential humanism of this faith, Eliot was not unmindful of forces and powers beyond man's control, the working of chance and the power of God. But he looked beyond both of these conceptions toward a fresh religious perspective:

There is, however, a third way of looking at human life and human history. This theory recognizes the part which chance plays in the actual course of events, and it also recognizes that God is the sovereign ruler of the universe; but it places the primary responsibility for human progress upon man himself, and it affirms the real possibility of man's consciously learning how to direct his own destiny so as to achieve increasingly the dreams and ideals which he cherishes.[2]

Thus in one paragraph Eliot illustrates the gradual transition from liberal theism to liberal humanism. God provides the natural conditions and limits of the setting in which man labors. God is always "there" to receive the prayers of those inclined to pray. But the real agency of man's progress is increasingly understood to be man himself, through the heroic exercise of his own willing responsibility. It is not surprising that succeeding generations of churchmen in this tradition should have less and less understanding of or inclination toward any kind of dependence upon God. Theological language itself, not to mention the faith it implies, steadily withers in the thought and speech of liberals.

The Unitarian church historian Sidney Mead observes that even the Christian sources of religious liberalism are to be sought at the humanist end of the religious spectrum, in Erasmus rather than the classic reformers, in the En-

[2] *Ibid.,* pp. 23-24.

lightenment of the eighteenth century, and in Romanticism and Transcendentalism in the nineteenth century. "The common element in this tradition," he says, "is the emphasis on man—his initiative and responsibility in the determination of his destiny—his 'destiny' usually being conceived as fulfillment somehow *in* history." [3]

If, as Eliot believed, the church must be made into "an efficient instrument" for our well-being through "thought and hard work and sacrificial loyalty," is there any place in such a church for the poor in spirit? A contemporary Unitarian minister answers quite bluntly in the negative:

The liberal church is not for the intellectually or emotionally faint-hearted, for those who wish to be soothed rather than stimulated on Sunday mornings. It is not the place to come to find strength but to develop it in oneself.

The primary task, then, of Unitarian humanism is to be itself, not to take cues from Christianity or from any other world religions. Nor is the task of Unitarian humanism, as I conceive it, to provide psychological equivalents for the emotional satisfactions offered by the various world religions. [4]

The tone is unfailingly heroic. Men must be bold to help themselves and one another. From out of the wells of their own courage they must draw their own refreshment. This is not to imply that liberal heroics are all of one kind. For some the emphasis is more intellectualist, stressing the primacy of scientific and pragmatic intelligence. Others are more nearly voluntarists (or, as we say today, "existentialists"); persons who are seeking to carve out new shapes of life and love without bondage either to older custom

[3] Sidney E. Mead, "An Address to Unitarians," *The Proceedings of the Unitarian Historical Society*, Vol. XVII, Part I, 1958.

[4] K. Arisian, "Unitarian Humanism," *Faith and Freedom*, Vol. XVII, Part I, Autumn 1963.

or to present-day scientific reasoning. There are also many levels of optimism or pessimism. Nearly everyone is required to preface even the most hopeful prognosis with the proviso "If we don't destroy ourselves first—" Some have a clear faith in the steady progress of democracy and the sciences toward an ever-finer life for all. Others, anxious about avoiding the dehumanization looming in a runaway technology, express faith in maintaining ties between man and his natural environment, thus hoping to provide a counterbalance to the abstract and artificial environment of urban man. All liberals today must carry within themselves a steady undertone of anxiety in face of the increasing involvement of the world in revolution and warfare. But in spite of different levels of optimism and pessimism the liberal seeks to defend and preserve a heroic frame of mind and demands of himself and his fellows increasing effort in that direction. The essential sermonic mood is exhortation. The essential appeal is to persons eager for challenge and concerned more for action than for comfort.

The Question of Tragedy

Thus far we have attempted to document Carl Wennerstrom's hunch that the doctrine of man in liberal theology is essentially heroic. The question now arises as to how far the analogy can be pushed. For instance, most Greek heroes were tragic heroes (Prometheus, Heracles, Achilles, Agamemnon, Oedipus). They were remembered not alone for their successes and powers but especially for their courage in face of adversity and in spite of ultimate disaster. The Greek mind looked upon catastrophe as perennial and expected to find highest wisdom in the very conditions of catastrophe. Defeat and death appeared as absolute affronts to human life and meaning unless, in the eloquence of grief and in the laws of cosmic justice revealed through suffering, some compensatory glory be discovered. Thus the Greeks accepted the inevitability of tragedy and endeavored to realize some spiritual gain thereby. Can we say as much for the heroic vein in the modern liberal doctrine of man?

The answer appears to be, as Wennerstrom has observed, that the liberal, being preoccupied with the active search for remedies, is at a loss in the face of irremediable tragedy. His whole inclination is to solve problems rather than bear them, to *do* rather than *be*. He is not spiritually disciplined to derive benefit, wisdom, even healing from situations in which there is precisely nothing to be done save to endure. He entertains the hope that there is always something to be done, that no tragedy has ultimate force. In these senses, the heroic ethos of the modern liberal is something less than heroic: it thrives mainly on strength, and is undercut in every time and place where strength fails and where resources, both intellectual and emotional, are exhausted. The tragic event, if it is viewed at all, is viewed negatively, not as the opportunity for some redemptive opening of heart and mind, but as a dreadful hiatus to be ignored in theory and to be transcended, as soon as possible, by remedial action. One suspects that this doctrine of man depends for its meaning and efficacy on faith in an unfailing human power to avoid or transcend every potentially tragic event by conscious planning and action. It becomes almost a matter of reproach for one to be reduced to helplessness especially if the fault is one's own. Nothing is so galling to the action-oriented mind as to see itself fail by its own miscalculations or to see the collapse of its hope in spite of all calculation.

It may be that just these kinds of tragic issues are building up from the accumulated effects of modern activistic and technological society. The rocket that might take us to the moon can also deliver a gigantic devastation. The very power to create and preserve life in geometrically increasing proportion and longevity leads to the specter of a lethally overcrowded planet. Our preoccupation with ever more ingenious means of communication increases also the means of the manipulation of information and the perversion of values, perhaps also thought control and the management of all motivations and opinons. The cry for security is answered by vast systems of authoritarian government, and the cry for freedom finds realization in young nations reckless with newfound weapons and peace-destroying convulsions.

The fact that the brave new world of scientific discovery and technological control is beginning to forecast its own tragedies is no reason for abandoning science or technology. The anxieties of our times would only increase if we failed to assume full responsibility for the forces our knowledge and ambition have unleashed. The question is not how to undo history but how to face the tragic possibilities of history without losing hope. As we come to realize the ever-increasing complexity of the difficulties we face in modern society—the slowness of remedies, the bitterness of struggle, the illiberal and fanatic energies not alone in others but lurking also within ourselves, the *hubris* of nations, and the manifold likelihood of consequent disaster—it becomes increasingly evident that some accounting for the reality and meaning of tragedy is long overdue in liberal theology's doctrine of man. Heroics are not enough unless, as the ancient Greeks understood, the fall of the hero is thoroughly contemplated. Just as Achilles understood that his heroic destiny to remain and fight the Trojan War was itself the prelude to his own early death, so we must contemplate the possibility that the heroic projects of modern civilization, for all their excellence and for all their claim upon our stewardship, may be the occasions for future disaster.

Perhaps the worst feature of a blatant heroics that is insensitive to tragedy is its pretentiousness. It exaggerates the psalmist's word that man is "a little lower than the angels" until man imagines himself to be his own angel and his own Redeemer. James Luther Adams, whose scholarship in the realms of liberal religious thought has made him sensitive to the characteristic forms of *hubris* in the liberal mind, finds a fatal pretentiousness rising in the eighteenth century. The Enlightenment's predilection "to live in accord with nature," he writes, "did not involve redemption from sin; it required rather that through the use of the powers of nature one should imitate the benevolence, the balance, the proportion, the symmetry of God. . . . The self-enclosed, bourgeois man, seemingly in control of himself and progressively gaining control of his environment, is his own god. His knees are frozen. Natural religion becomes merely the religion of success." [5] There is the suspicion that the confidence of the modern activist in the unfailing efficacy of analysis, education, reasoning, and controlled action is at least in part the temporary product of his socioeconomic privilege. His income and seeming security give him the illusion of self-directedness far beyond the actual facts of the case. He comes to think of his rational and decisive powers as autonomous and transcendent. He omits to prepare himself religiously for any time in life when circumstance may reduce him to helplessness.

[5] James Luther Adams, "Natural Religion and the 'Myth' of the Eighteenth Century," Dudleian Lecture, Harvard University, 1949-50. Published in *The Official Register of Harvard University*, Vol. 48, Sept. 20, 1951.

One would think that the vast changes in human experience since the eighteenth century would have effectively chastened the *hubris* of modern bourgeois man. And in some respects that is the case. The preoccupation of contemporary drama with pathos and meaninglessness has played havoc with the heroic image. So pervasive is the cynicism and despair of many educated as well as the uneducated men that the old liberal doctrine of self-sufficient man is in a struggle for its life. The command to heroism faces vast discouragements in our day, which were not so readily apparent to the confident optimists of a century or two ago. Amid these tensions it is tempting to promulgate a merely verbal heroism, ignoring how slow, exacting, and exhausting it is to nourish hope in the midst of involved and sacrificial action. The liberal who occupies a position in life of relative strength and security needs to be reminded that his command to "do better" misses the fact of real impoverishment of spirit in many persons and, in some cases, is an actual affront to the reduced fortunes and flagging morale even of his own friends and associates.

These developments are bringing about a different emphasis in the doctrine of man, one that does not denigrate heroic action but rather seeks to undergird it and bolster it by a faith more sensitive to the actual human condition. To enter even the vestibule of that faith, one must overcome compulsive attachment to rational tidiness and certainty, and accept the ambiguities, paradoxes, and mysteries of the human lot. One remains in the vestibule if this new acceptance is purely abstract and ideational, if it is no more than an intellectual acceptance of the fact that life is generally confusing and incomplete. Do not even the existentialists the same? The critical transition from the vestibule into the house occurs when one seeks to enter into, accept, and

137

share the woes of the persons who share his world. This does not mean that he should pretend to repeat the other person's actual suffering or deliberately make a false show of weakness. Rather it means that he does not let himself be frightened into an inept "social distance" by the fact of weakness, nor does he obscure the real situation by premature or ill-considered remedies, resolutions, or rationalizations. He deigns to be near, to listen to, to endure something of the very darkness from which the sufferer can at the moment find no escape.

Toward a Christian Humanism

The kind of sympathetic involvement we are describing is scarcely at all achievable simply by moral exhortation. One must be driven, as it were, from within. Augustine was bold to recognize this fact in his well-known phrase, "Command what Thou wilt and give what Thou commandest." His prayer recognizes that there are powers resident precisely within the difficult event which are sources of renewal to one who is open to them.

Toward the end of the first chapter Wennerstrom has written, "In the most confusing of all human paradoxes, weakness may prove to be strength, and strength, weakness." I believe that this is the starting point of the new conception of pastoral care he was seeking to formulate in the context of religious liberalism. It was not a program to denigrate strength as such, but rather the search for a new kind of strength or for a new way of recovering a temporarily exhausted strength. Even as he remained faithful to the best features of Unitarian humanism and heroism, he sought to find a transforming resource in the appropriation of an essentially Christian hope, the hope of new strength arising out of weakness. Here we see a vigorous humanism seeking to reestablish a link with the resources of its Christian past. This is an effort which owes nothing to the pious supposition that it is always good to revive neglected tradition in one's heritage. It is rather the bold surmise that the reconciliation of cultural elements which seem at first glance to be incompatible may issue in a new redemptive power in our own times. I believe Wennerstrom was moving toward a novel reconstruction of a Christian humanism.

To effect that reconstruction, the long-standing heroic individualism of the liberal must be qualified. He cannot rest secure in the rationalistic optimism of the nineteenth-century bourgeoisie, or in the consciousness of belonging to a scientific-technological élite with saving powers, or in the attitudes of defiance and rebellion characteristic of the many modes of contemporary existentialism. All of these tendencies toward self-isolation through intelligence, culture, expertness, or defiant anger leave the individual increasingly susceptible to despair as his social history becomes less manageable and more threatening. Individuality passes over into loneliness and independence is stripped of power.

If modern liberal man is to survive at all, he must acknowledge specific dependencies in his life, no matter how much this may hurt his pride or appear to be a regression to a more childlike mode of existence. He may then be open to the recognition that human fellowship per se is restorative quite apart from specific action programs or remedies. Those who are truly *with* him, having cast aside the embarrassments of helplessness, are already providing help. This in turn leads to the recognition that there is an analogy and a continuity between the rallying of diseased tissues to health and the gathering of a body of friends or of a body politic to its own restoration. A loving environment infuses its impulses to order and harmony into the disorders of an unbalanced body or mind. By such restorations the individual learns from experience, in a way no abstract idealism can teach, that his own being is essentially relational, that he is a part of larger organisms and societies which convey the power of renewal when he is open to them.

To acknowledge one's dependencies is equally important in the successful phases of life and in times of defeat. Every spurious form of heroics and most tendencies to "go it alone" are pathetic in their illusion and sinful in their ultimate effects. What is sinful is that enclosure of spirit which makes no effort to respond to other persons because of the mistaken notion that the cost of responding is an ultimate threat to one's own enjoyment and security. It is sinful to try to build a wall of security around a position of privilege, power, and intelligence as though those things are permanent and ultimate goals. The wider power is a common acceptance of stress, a common endurance, and a common energy toward renewal. The price is the acceptance of other woes beside one's own. In the degree to which a man fears to pay that price he actually reduces his power of living. If life is sacred, then any such reduction has an element of willful negation or sin. The transition away from sin rides on the willing acceptance of the realities of human pathos and tragedy and the actual venture of the person into the place of need.

The Initiative of Grace

There may be many civic-minded liberals who believe that their multiple community services and donations of money to this or that worthy cause constitute an effective participation in the human struggle. Although these impersonal movements for social welfare may be indispensable to the total health of the community, as a substitute for personal involvement, especially in the work of a minister, they can become misleading and idolatrous. They can insulate a person's mind to the fact of tragedy and tempt him to ignore the reality of that renewal which can only be known in the midst of tragedy. Not that one morbidly seeks for his own or another's suffering. Rather, in the power of religious faith one enters into proximity with whatever suffering is given in the expectation that the gathering of two or three or more can provide a mediation of grace. Just as the current racial struggles have progressed beyond abstract action into a new and dramatic interposing of the physical *body* in the battle for social justice, so in a new pastoral relationship, the bodily presence and carefully listening attention of the minister is primary. Without this presence, the many impersonal means of amelioration, for all their excellence, only increase the sense of loneliness in a depersonalized society. The use of taped telephone messages as alleged comfort for strangers in need seems merely to emphasize the comfortless quality of a depersonalized culture.

It is important for a minister to reach out to bereft persons with all the force of his concern, unembarrassed by the reality of suffering, undeterred by the fact of tragedy and its inevitability, unimpeded by his own lack of specific remedies or recommendations. Suffering in its initial impact isolates the sufferer and makes his environment seem alien. While he languishes in helplessness, the world hums along in its daily preoccupations: men are busy, children play, traffic moves, and birds sing. All this business-as-usual seems to the sufferer unfair, and he feels humanly adrift and

141

existentially unwanted. The arrival of human companion-ship which is truly companionate and compassionate means that some part of this seemingly alien world reaches in to him and rejoins him. If the so-called helper arrives in crisp uniform with orders, exhortations, and preconceived reme-dies, the "world" thus exemplified remains alien. It is a vi-sion of health impatient with suffering. But if some part of the healthy world can include suffering and be patient there-with, there is a true rejoining of the sufferer to the world, no matter how grievously the details of his suffering may persist.

May we not say that the first step in any kind of renewal is the faith that one is not disconnected from sources of power? Just as the individual is created in all the details of his individuality as an event within and dependent upon a society of events, so he is also *renewed*. When such a society, in addition to whatever remedies its wisdom may provide, maintains contact even in the depth of tragedy with its own sufferers, the effect is one of an initiating love reaching out to and preserving its own. Such action preserves an edge of sanity and humaneness even and especially in persons at the threshold of death or in moments of extreme loss.

In these ways I understand Carl Wennerstrom's expressed need for a revival among liberals of a doctrine of the Holy Spirit. It would seem that the minister who most fully, courageously, and unselfconsciously enters another's woe and mediates the gift of healing is an instance of the Spirit's visitation. Such events give authenticity to the witness that the Creator of Heaven and Earth also participates in the brokenness of human life and carries into that brokenness an undefeated hope and healing.

The suggestion of a revived doctrine of the Holy Spirit raises a new question for the renovation of the liberal's doctrine of man. Shall we say that the companion in suffering is purely a lonely individual giving himself in faithful companionship to other lonely individuals? Will the minister enter the sickroom or a house of tragedy in the tragic realization that he represents only his own human grief and concern? If so, it seems to me that a new pretension to specious heroism has crept into the event. The minister, by his own resolution, presumes to carry the burden himself and to see himself as the sole agent of renewal. Such a presumption is theologically inaccurate. The minister has little knowledge of, or command over, the total factors at work in a human crisis, the powers that dismay and the powers that give hope. The one gift he does have is his conviction that he represents the reality of healing per se, the very mystery of renewal. More by his acceptance of the fact of suffering than by any alleged remedy, he mediates that power. He and his parishioner are open to it, precisely because they are open to the extent of their own common need.

In these respects the relational doctrine of man includes a doctrine of grace or, if you will, a doctrine of the presence of the Holy Spirit. Whether the persons involved understand the locus of the Holy Spirit to be primarily the human community, or the wider community of the living and the dead, or the wider community of the created world, or the all-inclusive community of the love of God in which world, past history, and living men are contained, in any case, the meeting of man and man is in the name of an acknowledged holiness of which they are but parts. In that meeting, whether there are words of human communion or words of prayer or neither, there will also be generous silence, accepted in the shelter of a shared trust. The people will no longer be alone.

143

The Witness of the Biblical Tradition

A relational doctrine of man points back to cardinal insights in the biblical tradition. The covenants of the Old Testament were established not with individuals but with an entire people. And some of the prophets, notably Isaiah, understood the highest covenant to be ordained ultimately for all men. The Bible itself is largely a record of the vicissitudes of the bearers of the covenant, telling how they were brought into tragic events and how their faith in the renewal of grace for a people faithful to God's law enabled them to endure. The patriarch Jacob, being given an audience before Pharaoh, tells the king that the days of his own one hundred thirty years of life have been "few and evil" (Gen. 47:9). Jacob accurately summarizes his own story and makes no effort to gloss over the truth. But Jacob's story, analogous to the trials of Abraham before him or of Joseph and Moses and their descendants after them, is the very means of witnessing to the action of God among those who trust him; that is, among those who trust and follow his commands to righteousness in spite of every temptation to despair.

The Christian tradition adds new elements to the same essential story. The death of Jesus is no ultimate defeat to the fellowship of the disciples or to their trust in the love of man and God. When Jesus' power was released from the confinements of his own actual life, it became resident in a new community and constitutive of a new being for men. From the very depths of tragedy came new birth, symbolized in the resurrection faith of the disciples. A communion of men and women, faithful to the reality of renewal even in the presence of death, was established, and spread its influence over the world. In spite of every perversion of

144

the quality of this new being, in spite of the involvement of churchmen as well as unbelievers in ways alien to the church's teaching, this witness of man's relational fulfillment persists and haunts the western mind. It demands that the individual need not be surprised by the reduction of his life to trouble or tragedy. It asks that all such events not degenerate into a sinful spite toward man and the world. It commands those who are healthy and happy not to let either their euphoria of success or their anxiety for the security of success cut them off from the actual world where joy and pain are equally real and equally capable of receiving the gift of grace.

The church's witness affirms that the Creator's love enters into the realities of joy and pain, revealing in each an immortal power. That is to say, God, or his Holy Spirit, is incarnate in the actualities of natural events and in the events of human history, inspiring the genius of men and maintaining them in loving and mutual endurance when their genius fails and their lives are reduced to helplessness.

It should be clear that these several elements of a relational doctrine of man for liberal theology are not new in any absolute sense. They were founded in the early days of Jewish religious life and have appeared and reappeared in the long history of the Christian churches. However, in the burgeoning religious liberalism of the eighteenth and nineteenth centuries, these relational elements were driven into the background of liberal theology or else put into total eclipse. The pendulum of history now swings back toward a renewed consciousness of tragedy. And all persons concerned with religious meaning, especially Unitarians and other like-minded liberals, find themselves at a crossroads. Shall the heroic spirit become so impersonal in operation and so strident in its self-advancement that it obscures the

145

fact of tragedy and prepares the way for new despair and a steady transition toward pure pathos? Or shall men discover a new birth of the love of God because they have been willing to be mediators of that love, especially and chiefly in times of tragedy? In Carl Wennerstrom's ministry, in his persistent studies and experience—perhaps even in the shock of his tragic early death—the force of that new wisdom became clear and eloquent. It is a word suited to our needs and hopefully destined to become characteristic of our times.

LIBERAL AND EXISTENTIAL DIMENSIONS OF PASTORAL CARE

Charles R. Stinnette

In his *Leaves from the Notebook of a Tamed Cynic*, Reinhold Niebuhr wrote in 1929, as he reflected upon his ministry to a working-class group in Detroit:

It seems pathetic to me that liberalism has too little appreciation of the tragedy of life to understand the cross and orthodoxy insists too much upon the uniqueness of the sacrifice of Christ to make the preaching of the cross effective.[1]

Niebuhr's comment grew out of his firsthand experience of the social evils of a burgeoning industrial city whose brutality and callousness seemed to refute the liberal estimate of man. Nevertheless, Niebuhr's subsequent theological development was rooted in a liberalism seasoned by tragedy and an understanding of the cross made relevant and universal by the Detroit experience.

Carl Wennerstrom experienced the same shock of recognition in his work as a liberal hospital chaplain. In his unfin-

[1] Reinhold Niebuhr, *Leaves from the Notebook of a Tamed Cynic* (Chicago: Willett and Clark, 1929), p. 8.

147

ished dissertation he stated his conviction that it is the minister himself who must serve as "the re-creative agent in the parishioner's life of pain," and yet, he reflected, the one who finds himself attempting to fulfill this mission within the liberal perspective acts in inexplicable ways to thwart and repel the person in need. Why?

Carl Wennerstrom developed the hypothesis that the "heroic" motif in liberal thought had crowded out the notion of man in his weakness. He proposed to explore the emergent development in pastoral care derived largely from depth psychology and the sociology of knowledge in which the liberal doctrine of man would take into account the contradictions and discontinuities actually experienced by fallible man.

He was not able to complete his reconstructive task. He sensed the note of change, however, which is upon us today in the new context of pastoral care, with its radical demand for the recasting of theology.

One need only read the "essay with exhibits" which Clebsch and Jaekle have collected in order to discern the long struggle of the theology of pastoral care within the Babylonian captivity of dogmatic theology.[2] Long after Schleiermacher opened the gates to the inductive method in theology, the task of theological ordering in pastoral care was still relegated to "practics." Contemporary history is changing this, aided and abetted by social change. Seward Hiltner's *Preface to Pastoral Theology* presented us with a charter for organizing pastoral theology in terms of function; and subsequent theological developments seem to reinforce this direction.[3] Thus, Paul Lehmann has recently empha-

[2] William A. Clebsch and Charles R. Jaekle, *Pastoral Care in Historical Perspective* (Englewood Cliffs, N.J.: Prentice-Hall, 1964).
[3] Seward Hiltner, *Preface to Pastoral Theology* (Nashville: Abingdon Press, 1958).

sized the functional character of all theology, as distinguished from speculative disciplines.[4] Theology is *responsive*, not merely *reflexive*, he holds. It is oriented not toward metaphysics but toward ethics, toward an implementation and integration of the subject of theology in the life of the congregation.

The twofold impact of the new world view promulgated by science and what Harvey Cox calls the "epoch of the secular city" has radically affected the context and the work of pastoral care.[5] All theology is being forced to recast its cognitive symbols in light of the fluid relation of person and milieu. Indeed, theologians are being forced to take up the task of a theology of revolution in the midstream of change. It is this reconstructive reworking of theology en route and the intellectual challenge of our time which provide the new climate of pastoral care.

Three Currents Affecting Pastoral Care

As an introductory summary I propose now to examine briefly three main currents in contemporary experience and thought affecting pastoral care.

First, there is the experienced personal threat of the loss of identity in the midst of rapid social change. The experience of anxiety, alienation, and anomie are reflected in modern man's consuming interest in the question, "Who Am I?" It is common knowledge in psychiatry that the problem of identity is reshaping the methods and goals of psychotherapy itself. Modern man is almost frantic in his

[4] Paul Lehmann, "The Formative Power of Particularity," *Union Seminary Quarterly Review*, XVIII (1962), 210.

[5] Harvey G. Cox, *The Secular City* (New York: Macmillan Paperbacks ed., 1964).

search for an identity that he may call his own, one that yields some sense of unity within continuity and the task of mastery. But it is just here that psychiatry alone proves unable to supply what is finally needed. Accelerated social change with its twin processes of pluralism and urbanization tends to antiquate and undermine the very means by which identity is achieved. Allen Wheelis, while pointing out that values determine goals and goals define identity, sketches the disquieting dilemma for contemporary man:

If out of the multitudinous choices of modern life he commits himself to certain values and with them builds a durable identity, he is apt to lose contact with a rapidly changing world; if he does not commit himself, but maintains an alert readiness to move with the current, he suffers a loss of the self. Not knowing what he stands for, he does not know who he is.[*]

Wheelis clearly indicates that the identity crisis experienced by modern man points to the conflict between institutional values and the instrumentalities of social change. As the reality of this precarious and conflictual nature of human identity emerges, modern man is forced more and more to see himself in terms of a process of becoming rather than as a fixed entity. Maturity itself becomes a matter of openness to change in oneself as one responds to social innovation. But the necessity of unity and continuity within change is no less a paramount human need. How may we reinterpret baptism and other identity symbols concerned with the "rites of passage" in such a way that man is enabled to claim his freedom in this new age? This task is a stirring challenge to pastoral care today.

[*] Allen Wheelis, *The Quest for Identity* (New York: W. W. Norton, 1958), p. 129.

Second, the dynamic and interacting character of human identity suggests that personal knowledge itself is more action-centered than either rationalism or empiricism have ever been willing to admit. Knowing is an active rather than a passive process. Descartes's formula is, in fact, reversed—"I am, therefore I think"—if one's existence is, indeed, recognized for what it is, i.e., continuing encounter between personal agents rather than one long, solitary vigil to shut out the world.

Where history is important, action as the context of knowing and reflection will also be important. For the word *action* (praxis) is a distinctively human word. "In a strict sense of the term," John MacMurray writes, "only a person can 'act' or in a proper sense 'do' anything." [7] Action refers to human agency, and the cognitive processes involve the union of intention and act (symbolization, Gestalt, etc.) as well as judgment. Indeed, human knowing in its most profound sense is transformative as well as cognitive. Bernard E. Meland has described revelation as "an event which transforms or recreates man's sense of knowing and brings to judgment what man's own reason has wrought." In this context he concludes, "Revelation is the encounter with the depth of God's reality in history, an event which man's reason or experience did not, or even could not, apprehend on its own initiative." [8]

A reminder, however, is in order here. Since the cognitive symbols of both revelation and reason are shaped by the social milieu in which they function, man's knowledge,

[7] John MacMurray, *The Self As Agent* (New York: Harper Brothers, 1958), p. 89.

[8] Bernard E. Meland, *The Realities of Faith* (New York: Oxford University Press, 1962), p. 171.

whether in revelation or reason, is always conditioned and partial. It is branded with the mark of its own history and time. Freud once said that anatomy is destiny, but he was only partly right. The psychosocial evaluation of anatomy *in history* is destiny. Even more important is the realization that as a historical creature man is both the product of and the creator of his own destiny and that he understands the meaning of history only as he undertakes the task of changing it.

If knowing is an active, participative process that involves change in that which is known as well as in the knower himself, the task of pastoral care must be extended to include appropriate change in the psychosocial milieu of troubled persons. The one-to-one relation in pastoral counseling must be understood as but one aspect of change in a whole matrix of relationships and values that are ultimately determinative of its effectiveness. Indeed, the strategy of pastoral care in this light calls for more attention to family- and community-centered activities in which therapy and understanding are by-products of the effort to solve problems and to initiate change in the social order itself. Psychological observers have been struck by the fact that problems of delinquency and deviant behavior have diminished among minority groups actively engaged in the struggle for civil rights.

The third current in contemporary experience and thought affecting pastoral care may be described as a pragmatic attitude. I wish to distinguish this attitude from the technical term designating the philosophy of pragmatism. While the pragmatic attitude which I have in mind does share pragmatism's approach toward truth, i.e., that truth is not a stagnant property inherent in an idea but rather some-

152

thing that happens to it, pragmatism tends to be identified with Darwinian naturalism, which finally understands all phenomena in terms of the genetic model. The pragmatic attitude, on the other hand, approaches experience with greater latitude, accepting the admonition of the phenomenologists first to let the phenomena communicate with us in terms of their own integrity. The pragmatic attitude eschews methodological imperialism. It thus offers a meeting ground for the various intellectual disciplines, which at least insures the possibility that their respective subject matters shall be seen initially as entities before they are reduced to a function of other perspectives.

It occurs to me that the pragmatic attitude has made possible not only the study and research into the phenomena of religion, but also many other aspects of human behavior hitherto excluded by narrow empiricism. Hence Max Scheler's studies in sympathy, resentment, and repentance, or Dorothy Lee's anthropological studies of symbolization in primitive cultures, are only two of the illustrations of the rich opportunities now open and available for study.

The pragmatic attitude opens new frontiers in pastoral care as an expansion of an already established model for research in clinical pastoral education. Anton Boisen encouraged ministers to study the "living human documents" of theology in the persons who are in crisis and illness. It soon turned out, however, that the study of others, while fulfilling a professional role, necessarily involved also the study of oneself. Examined experience, including an ongoing critical appraisal of oneself, has become an important adjunct in clinical pastoral education. The research-minded reader will recognize immediately that the expected result of such examined experience and self-appraisal represents an important element in psychosocial control.[9] The theological researcher who is sensitive to his own tendency toward "selective" perception and interpretation of data has already taken an important first step in controlling this variable in research.

It appears, therefore, that the already established resources of the clinical pastoral education movement represent assets not only in strengthening the professional competency of ministry but also in providing a wider selection of subjects for research hitherto discouraged by limited empiricism.[10] Thus the role and function of images of "depth" (as replacing spatial images) in communicating modern man's perception of himself in religious terms is but one area that seems to invite research attention. Another is the question which Harvey Cox has raised, i.e., are the existential queries of Tillich (guilt, death and meaninglessness) in fact being asked by contemporary secular man? [11]

Examined experience is itself a first step in research. I am suggesting that it is a foundation for more intensive efforts, afforded by the pragmatic attitude, which should enrich the discipline of pastoral care immeasurably.

The New Context of Theology

The intellectual currents that we have just sketched are rooted in the new perception of reality in modern history, which has moved from a static world view to a more dynamic understanding of the space-time continuum. It is

[9] See GAP (Group for the Advancement of Psychiatry) Report #42, "Some Observations on Controls in Psychiatric Research," May, 1959.

[10] See David Jenkins, "Concerning Theism," in *The Honest to God Debate* (Paperback ed.; London: SCM, 1963), p. 202.

[11] Cox, *Secular City*, p. 78.

a world of emerging realities, of continuities rather than discontinuities, where knowledge is a function of inter-action between subject and object, and the concept of im-mutable substance has disappeared. John Dewey charac-terized this new Copernican revolution as conceiving of the mind not as a spectator but as a participant knower in change. Ideal ends, he held, cannot be cultivated apart from attention to the actual means used in achieving them. Hence "the problem of restoring integration and cooperation between man's beliefs about the world in which he lives and his beliefs about the values and purposes that should direct his conduct is the deepest problem of modern life." [12]

There are three principal aspects of this new context in theology, which will be dealt with in turn.

First, coming to terms with the new Weltbild. The task of restoring integrity between the new world view of science and the ultimate values and meaning of faith has occupied a central place in theological reconstruction in recent history. Whether this vast effort has succeeded in providing a uni-versally acceptable resolution, which Dewey hoped for, is another matter. However, both the wide interest and shock occasioned by the appearance of the little book *Honest to God* [13] leads one to the impression that Dewey's appeal for moral and intellectual integrity strikes a responsive chord in contemporary man.

John A. T. Robinson makes it clear that in his book he is simply giving a brief summary of some theological cur-

[12] John Dewey, *The Quest for Certainty* (Paperback ed.; New York: Capricorn Books, 1960 [1929]), p. 255. See the whole of Chapter X, "The Construction of Good," for Dewey's understanding of the moral imperatives implicit in the new world view.

[13] John A. T. Robinson, *Honest to God* (Paperback ed.: Philadel-phia: Westminster Press, 1963).

rents that have been under discussion for at least a generation. It is also clear that he is disturbed about the problem of communicating the Christian faith in a world that has been so radically transformed by science and technology. His theological mentors reflect this apologetic concern also. Thus, in addition to his own conclusions as a New Testament scholar, Robinson draws particularly upon the thought of Tillich, Bultmann, and Bonhoeffer.

Dietrich Bonhoeffer has become a symbol for the demands of a revolutionary theology, conveyed in part by his twin slogans, "Man come of age" and "religionless Christianity." His *Letters and Papers from Prison* as he waited out the ordeal of World War II—a wait cut short by his own execution just prior to its end—reflect theologically the radical austerity and pared-down existence which must have been his daily lot.

"God is teaching us," he wrote, "that we must live as men who can get along very well without him." [14] It should be made clear, however, that the word *religion* as used by Bonhoeffer tends to refer to a private God who keeps man safe from disenchantment, a *deus ex machina* for magically solving all of man's problems "on call" and one who confirms man in his complacency. It need hardly be said that what Bonhoeffer calls "religion," Jesus called "sin." Indeed, the biblical protest against utilitarian religion reveals its ultimate logic in the empty cross where God hides himself from human manipulation. Thus removed, the hidden God no longer provides support for man's infantile desires which he calls religion. Man is left on his own—forced to come of age—as Christ was left alone in Gethsemane and, later, on

[14] Eberhard Bethge, ed. (New York: Macmillan Paperbacks ed., 1962 [1953]), p. 219.

the cross. Thus it is that man, come of age and seasoned in faith, is sent back into the world without the purse or script of the old securities. As Theodore Wedel has commented:

We have to act and to make decisions in the World "as if God did not exist," but the decisions are nevertheless *before* God. The matter of prayer is supplied by the world—by the engagement pad and the telephone.[15]

If Bonhoeffer's passion was to fight religion in the name of radical faith, Bultmann's effort has been to recast theology as the methodological exposition of self-understanding on the premise of faith. As a New Testament scholar, Bultmann recognizes biblical imagery and metaphor as having been shaped by the popular cosmology of the day. Every age must do its own demythologizing—even the New Testament writers!

Bultmann proposes to replace the crude spatial metaphors of a three-decker world by the intelligible language of the modern world, while retaining the essential meaning conveyed by biblical language. Methodologically, he finds the key to the transformation of the biblical message in existentialism. Man as man must deal with the agonizing questions of historical existence, e.g., Who am I? Who are you? What are we doing here? The unflinching pursuit of these questions on the premise of faith "here and now" leads ultimately to the revelation that one lives from grace. "Belief in God," Bultmann once wrote, "is the courage which gives utterance to this 'nevertheless'—'nevertheless I

[15] Theodore O. Wedel, review of *Honest to God*, by J. A. T. Robinson, *Episcopalian*, August, 1963.

am continually with thee: Thou hast holden me by my right hand.' " [16]

An underlying motif in the constructive theological response to the changing *Weltbild* is the question, "How are we to communicate the meaning of Christian faith in such a world?" Modern man is, as George MacLeod has put it, "earthed" and "materially environed." A positive acceptance of the fact that we are "enmeshed in this materialism" and theology, understood as the effort to interpret this process, has characterized the view of Christian naturalism. Where Bultmann emphasizes a radical historicity ("History begins with awakening consciousness of man, with the break with nature" [17]), naturalism tends to see man as continuous with nature.

A core problem emerges, then, concerning God's relationship to the world, particularly as that relationship is centered in man's consciousness of himself as a historical creature, i.e., one conscious of being enmeshed in nature, yet curiously free. Without abandoning his naturalism, the theologian here finds assistance in the concepts of "emergent evolution" and Whitehead's "process thought." There follows the rigorous effort to think through how it is possible for God to act in the world and remain God, even as man is "materially environed" and yet free. John B. Cobb, Jr., summarizes the costly discipline involved in this enterprise:

Of course, such reflection must eschew appeal to any authority not recognized outside the church, such as Scripture, revelation, tradition or personal religious experience. It must be as thorough-

[16] Rudolf Bultmann, *Essays: Philosophical and Theological*, trans. James C. G. Grieg (London: SCM Press, 1955), p. 6.

[17] Bultmann, *History and Eschatology* (New York: Harper & Row, 1957), p. 76.

ly open to evidence as any other mode of thinking, and it must unreservedly risk its own basic vision in the process. Indeed, it can justify itself only by showing that Christian faith, more than any other perspective, dares to risk the surrender of all security in the interest of truth.[18]

The word *risk* appears often in contemporary theology. Perhaps the theologians have taken to heart Kierkegaard's warning that faith is irremediable risk, a leap in trust. Certainly Paul Tillich puts risk at the heart of his theology. It is Tillich, apparently, who inspires John Robinson to describe Christianity as "humanism within a mystery;" theologically, a move beyond naturalism and supernaturalism. Tillich would agree that faith has no real purpose where the direct (or literal) Christ replaces the indirect. All events are grounded in God as being itself, and the uniqueness of the Christ event is its transparent revelation of the ground of being. The concept of "depth" replaces supernaturalism, and man, through faithful response to the Gestalt of grace vouchsafed ultimately in the event of Christ, is enabled to center his quest for the unambiguous life. In affirming the necessity of risk in coming to terms with the open world of dynamism, change, and participative knowledge (as opposed to closed, archaic structures), Tillich's whole theology is pivoted on love as the ontological foundation of change. "Love," he writes, "transforms the moralisms of authority into a morality of risk. Love is creative, and creativity includes risk." [19]

[18] "Christian Natural Theology and Christian Existence," *The Christian Century*, March 3, 1965, p. 266. See also Cobb, *A Christian Natural Theology* (Philadelphia: Westminster Press, 1965).

[19] Paul Tillich, "Moralism and Morality: Theonomous Ethics," *Theology of Culture*, ed. Robert C. Kimball (New York: Oxford University Press, 1959), p. 145.

Second, toward a theology of social change. The theological response which we have just sketched is marked by the common aim of recasting theology in the light of the new *Weltbild.* While strongly influenced by this structural reformulation of theology, another response is characterized by its concern with the practical, ethical, and sociological consequences of the new world. "The starting point for any theology of the church today," Harvey Cox writes, "must be a theology of social change. The church is first of all a responding community, a people whose task is to discern the action of God in the world and to join in his work." [20]

Cox proposes to set the processes of secularization and urbanization within a theological perspective. Secularization is defined as the deliverance of man from religion and from all metaphysical control over his reason or language.[21] The secular city is the instrument of this liberation. Anonymity and mobility are among its treasures, freeing man from overtaxing I-Thou relations. Here man is encouraged to come of age, to accept maturation and responsibility, and to turn away from juvenile dependencies, i.e., "mythical meanings and cultic afterglows that marked him during the 'religious' stage of history." [22] Cox finds the sources of secularization in biblical religion; in the disenchantment of nature initiated in the creation, the desacralization of politics in Exodus, and the deconsecration of values in the Sinai covenant. Cox's radical this-world-only perspective frees the church, he believes, from encumbrances and sets its proper task in the world—"how to come to political terms with the emergent technical reality which engulfs us." Cox concludes

[20] Cox, *Secular City,* p. 105.
[21] *Ibid.,* p. 18. While "secularization" is liberating, "secularism" as an ideology is a new closed world view.
[22] *Ibid.,* p. 217.

that the political mode of activity must replace metaphysical theology.

While Cox's socioethical analysis has many elements in common with such definitive theologians as Reinhold Niebuhr, H. Richard Niebuhr, and Paul Lehmann, one important aspect of his thought is markedly different, i.e., he appears to ignore the crucial problem of theological anthropology. This defect appears in other socioethical analysts whose proposals for renewal and relevance in church and ministry are provocative and highly significant, but lacking in that realism about man which is one of the foundation stones of the revival of theology in our day.[23]

Why this lack of realism concerning man *as man?* One is led to suspect that an uncritical transformation of sociological description into anthropological norms is taking place. Man is exhorted to become what he is *sociologically*, but neither the norm nor the human problem of becoming "fully of age" is examined critically. Meanwhile, the en-

[23] Both Cox and Gibson Winter, in *The New Creation as Metropolis* (New York: The Macmillan Co., 1963), have provided timely and significant proposals for the renewal of ministry in the urban world. Both, however, appear to project the "urban man" as the ideal man who appears on the scene with sociological predictableness. He is post-primitive, post-town and avant-garde urban. He requires neither cultic nor confessional worship because he belongs to a world which possesses new "cognitive skills" and "verbal abilities." But this ideal man, like Minerva, arrives on the scene already mature—man come of age. How does one discover this man? What is the relation of normative and descriptive efforts to locate this man? What of the problems of maturing, even beyond the age of maturity? For that matter, what of the person in the person-society equation? The socioethicists appear to dichotomize man anew. Perhaps Kierkegaard is not authoritative in social ethics, but I am reminded of his insistence that sin enters the world through the individual, i.e., each man must recognize and claim his own responsible guilt, whether in public or private spheres. The weight of social science tends to divert responsibility away from the person.

161

during human problem is revealed in the "caricature of what might have been" discovered by depth psychology. Man, including emancipated man, is not an unqualified success story. The liberation of secularism will alter the context but not the reality of this problem. As one patient who was struggling back to responsible maturity said to Chaplain Ernest E. Bruder, " 'Free to choose' doesn't necessarily mean 'able' to choose, you know." [24]

The peril as well as the promise of man's technological emancipation represents an enduring insight into human nature emphasized particularly by Reinhold Niebuhr and supported clinically by the experience of those who are engaged in therapy. However, Cox's *Secular City* is a sharp reminder for church and ministry that it is a peril which cannot be evaded. Perhaps the cutting edge of secularization finds theological (and psychological) support in H. Richard Niebuhr's radical monotheism. Here all values are both relative and judged in the "One beyond all the many whence the many derive their being." [25] Prophetic faith views all values, religion, culture, security, etc., in the light of the command, "You shall worship the Lord your God, and him only shall you serve" (Luke 4:8).

Indeed the practical task that faces the church and its ministry today finds sympathetic theological support in both H. Richard Niebuhr and Paul Lehmann.[26] Both emphasize the indicative rather than the imperative mood in ethics. Both regard an assessment of what is happening as the decisive first step in deciding what should be done. Both

[24] Ernest E. Bruder, *Ministering to Deeply Troubled People* (Englewood Cliffs, N.J.: Prentice-Hall, 1963), p. 32.

[25] H. Richard Niebuhr, *Radical Monotheism and Western Culture* (New York: Harper & Row, 1960), p. 32.

[26] Paul Lehmann, *Ethics in a Christian Context* (New York: Harper & Row, 1963).

would agree with Cox that a theology of change is a crucial need today. Indeed Niebuhr interprets the genius of Protestantism as its capacity to realize the active nature of faith in change:

It has not sought to convince a speculative, detached mind of the existence of God, but has begun with actual moral and religious experience, with the practical reasoning of the existing person rather than with the speculative interests of the detached mind.[27]

Third, toward a psychosocial modality for pastoral care. That deeper investment in human existence which is the prevailing note in contemporary theology will find its geography, so to speak, in the psychosocial matrix of man's being and becoming. The immediate problem is one of self-understanding on the part of any caring or therapeutic agent. How shall he, through his action, become interior to the person or group whom he proposes to cure? Here Harry Stack Sullivan's "one genus hypothesis," which developed out of his work with disturbed persons, may prove helpful. Sullivan assumed that persons are much more simply human than otherwise, that the sick and the well have more in common than their differences. The very possibility of therapy is rooted in a capacity for empathic participation in another's need by means of the instrumentality of one's own personhood. The agent of care has within his own fund of registered experience an immediate resource for interpersonal communication.

Further reflection on this one genus hypothesis leads to the additional insight that every man is the carrier of a particular developmental history that has evolved within

[27] H. R. Niebuhr, *Radical Monotheism*, p. 116.

a unique social context. Every man bears the mark of his own psychosocial history. George Herbert Mead explored the dialectical dimensions of this psychosocial matrix in his seminal study, *Mind, Self and Society*.[28] Mead insisted that the mind is a "social fact" which is reciprocally related to the correlative emergence of language and selfhood. Its expressive modes are social and symbolic transformations of the logic of psychosocial history. It follows that a ministry which expects to become both relevant and transformative in human history must look to its own reservoir of registered experience as a first step in therapeutic intervention.

"To be a self," H. Richard Niebuhr has written, "is to have a god; to have a god is to have history, that is, events connected in a meaningful pattern; to have one god is to have one history. God and the history of selves in community belong together in inseparable union." [29] If to be a self is to have a history as anchored in some self-transcending identity (i.e., God), selfhood also requires the understanding that the human link between persons provides its own means of renewal. Like the marriage contract, this human link is capable of enduring "for better for worse, for richer for poorer, in sickness and health" where the intention "to love and to cherish" is present.

Indeed, the psychosocial constitution of human personality revealed by the behavioral sciences represents a crucial step in reconstructing a theological anthropology, and its consequent therapeutic modalities. Whatever may be said about man (i.e., that he is a rational, political, or symbol-using animal), it must be recognized that he is a *socius*. His

[28] George Herbert Mead, *Mind, Self and Society*, ed. Charles W. Morris (Chicago: The University of Chicago Press, 1934).
[29] H. Richard Niebuhr, *The Meaning of Revelation* (New York: The Macmillan Co., 1941), p. 80.

reality is socially matrixed which, from the beginning, finds him already involved in the bands of mutual responsibility. "Existence is a personal relation of the self in the community of selves," writes Hans Frei. He adds, "Its categories of reflection and decision are ethical rather than natural. Communication is thought and decision 'within' rather than 'about' existence." [30] Man finds himself already "earthed" and matrixed in a network of human relationships. The question for man, therefore, is not "What is relationship?" but "How shall I respond to relationship?"

Thus the task of pastoral care becomes one of gaining theological perspective upon the psychosocial modalities appropriate for human communication. The word *modality* suggests action and a dynamism of underlying intentions which manifest themselves in action. The person is constituted by such actions which have been appropriated and registered as a fund of socially meaningful symbols. He who proposes to intervene in another's life as a helper must first become aware of the struggle within his own history to find these appropriate modalities. Ministry should be viewed, then, as a matter of continual revisitation and reflection upon experience as a theater of simultaneous possibilities. While therapeutic modes are being reshaped by human needs, their significance is illumined and reinterpreted by theological self-understanding.

The Liberation of Pastoral Care

We began this discussion by citing Carl E. Wennerstrom's courage in facing the necessary reformulation of liberal views

[30] Hans Frei, "Niebuhr's Theological Background," *Faith and Ethics: The Theology of H. Richard Niebuhr,* ed. Paul Ramsey (New York: Harper & Row, 1957), p. 15.

of man, a necessity that grew out of reflection upon his pastoral work. It is significant that theological reformulation here was initiated in practical experience. A whole segment of man's existence, his experienced "weakness," had been ignored by "heroic" estimates derived largely from an idealistic anthropology. This rationalistic denial of man's fallibility is inherent in an archaic theological method that fails to take into account the immediate data of human experience in framing anthropological statements. Human complexity has a way of showing up "the fallacy of misplaced concreteness," as Whitehead noted. The question "What is man?" tends to result in such a fallacy if in our answer we are permitted to ignore the particularity of that question, "Who am I?" Jesus admonished the women of Jerusalem to weep not for him but for themselves and their children. "If only we can weep for ourselves as *men*," Reinhold Niebuhr has commented, "We need not weep for ourselves as *man!*" [31]

It should not be overlooked, however, that Carl Wennerstrom found support for theological innovation *within* the liberal tradition which he criticized. Indeed the inductive method in theology, introduced by Schleiermacher and emphasizing as it does a role of theological discovery *in experience,* represents a significant step forward in the liberation of pastoral care from captivity to dogmatic theology. Anton Boisen was standing on this same newly won freedom when he insisted that the "living human documents" of theology—persons—must be studied firsthand. We have already noted that the present theological mood reenforces this deeper immersion in human existence.

[31] Reinhold Niebuhr, *Beyond Tragedy* (New York: Charles Scribner's Sons, 1938), p. 168. The New Testament reference is Luke 23:28.

An expression of this new freedom is the insistent note that history is the locus of caring work rather than some special sphere which may be labeled religion. Hence pastoral care is freed from its special mentality characterized by religious acts for work in the world. It must become a ministry of care through history to those whose history is burdened with care, the embarrassed, the hurt, and the alienated. If pastoral care is to fulfill its task, it must recover its prophetic authority. It must transform the burden of care into a zeal for change and for new horizons of meaning. The form of ministry is represented by Christ's relation to troubled persons *as interior to their history*. Its goal, however, is the reopening of persons to that bending of God's kingdom toward human history which renews and transfigures the human enterprise. The liberation of pastoral care is marked, therefore, by a consensus with biblical religion that one understands history (both individually and socially) in the effort to change it, i.e., as a prophetic agent who acts as interior to its processes.

Carl Wennerstrom was influenced by the liberal spirit which insisted that prophetic religion is a here and now affair. It welcomes new occasions and new challenges to old forms. It recognizes that conflict and change are central rather than accidental in human encounter. The depth dimension in personality made accessible in psychoanalysis confirms this centrality of conflict. It also convinced Carl Wennerstrom that liberalism has a stake in recovering this depth dimension in its pastoral care of persons. Immediate theological support for this conviction was warmly present in his friend and teacher, Bernard E. Meland. In many ways Meland represents the new stance in liberal theology. He has responded to the rediscovery of "depth" and its role in shaping the new formative images of our day. He has widened the liberal theological framework to include what psychology has discovered about the continuing influence of irrational forces in personality or physics about discontinuity as well as continuity. Thus Meland has noted that "depth implies a relationship and a complexity of meaning which defies ready observation or analysis." [32] It follows, then, that man's experience of depth imposes some limits on the notion that reason is the sole arbitrator of truth. That encounter with depth also casts new light on the mode of revelation. To encounter depth, Meland insists, is one way of describing man's encounter with God's reality in history.

The recognition that history rather than religious spheres is the locus of pastoral acts is grounded in the theological conviction that God is acting through crisis and change *to make life more human*, as Paul Lehman has put it. The context of pastoral care is shifted to existence itself, and the ministry is freed to address itself to man as man. The central importance of existence as experienced freedom, therefore, represents another step in the liberation of pastoral care. Its task is not so much the care of a flock, as in some pastorally stable society, as the nurture of "a free man's worship," to use a phrase from Bertrand Russell.

If man's humanity is revealed in Christ, man is indeed free for freedom. Pastoral care, then, is rooted in the realization of that freedom in man's personal and social existence. Its method is practical and reflective rather than the application of preexisting formulations to present experience. It proceeds by the integration of perceived meaning (i.e., faith symbols as immersed in experience) with appropriate means of their realization. The ministry of care is found not

[32] Meland, *Faith and Culture* (New York: Oxford University Press, 1953), p. 39.

as a "caretaker" but as a participant in the ongoing process of theological reflection. This focus upon the existential and integrative character of pastoral care is paralleled in the emphasis upon autonomy and freedom in ego psychology, where attention is turned more and more to the adaptational and integrative functions of the ego in action.

A prevailing motif in contemporary theology expressed by Bonhoeffer is the insistence that to be a Christian is first of all to be a man. But to be a man is to experience existence as a particular man whose history and self-understanding are linked through the history operative in him here and now. To be a man is to know finitude and weakness in the very act of self-transcending choice. To be a man is to know both the good I would do and the evil that I do, and yet to act responsibly in the moral and social issues which confront one day by day. It is to live with the necessary tension between public and personal realms and to resist the temptation fo flee into either as ways of escaping the existential demands of history as now lived. Here again the liberation of pastoral care appears as a rediscovery of essential humanity. Is not this the primary ministry of Christ? To participate in such a ministry is to discover what it means to be a man for others: It is to be a man as reflectively *transfigured under the healing revelation* of God in Christ.

Ministry as Prophetic Servanthood

Man's new freedom calls for a ministry of prophetic servanthood in the world. Its imperative is rooted in the very fact that the burden of care (sorge) is a cry of distress that is also a summons to help. The work of ministry is the transformation of that care into caring. The new freedom and the new context of pastoral care are represented in man's knowledge of the psychosocial dynamics which provide channels of communication and care. This knowledge equips man with ways of reflecting upon his own interiority, while becoming interior to others as an agent of change. But having ways of change does not alone provide the motive for change. Rather it is in the recognition that *in Christ* signifies that means and ends are united. The meaning of Christ's ministry is inseparable from the mode of its appearance in history. The question "Lord, when did we see thee hungry . . . a stranger . . . naked . . . sick or in prison?" has only one answer; "as you did it unto one of the least of these my brethren, you did it to me" (Matt. 25:37-40). In his ministry Christ is always identified with our primordial brother (man himself) whose affliction is both the occasion and the summons for divine healing.

Ministry, then, is man's faithful response to human stress as the bearer of prophetic meaning. In psychosomatic medicine we have learned to regard illness as a reminder of the purpose of life. Symptoms reveal as well as conceal the wider meaning of the patient's disorder. "Symptoms are dubiously useful errors, with which a sufferer hides some truth from himself," Philip Rieff has observed.[33] This insistence upon relating symptom to human intention, whether conscious or unconscious, restores ethical and social concerns to the whole conception of illness. Furthermore, if no man is an island unto himself, his symptoms point beyond his own character structure to the social matrix which bred his sickness. Society and self are reciprocally related in human interaction, and the dialectic between these two

[33] Philip Rieff, *Freud: The Mind of the Moralist* (Anchor Books; Garden City, N. Y.: Doubleday & Co., 1961), p. 12.

170

poles provides a way of viewing the moral climate as well as the dynamics of a given milieu. Scapegoating in a family where one member may be identified as the deviant yet who conveniently acts out the ambivalent wishes of other members, is a ready illustration of such a psychosocial climate. We mean to suggest that one cannot fully understand human stress without taking into account his moral and prophetic climate.

The prophet is a seer, one who speaks the word of God as both interior to a people's history and one in communion with God.[34] It is within the course of his participation in a common history that the prophet's eyes are opened to God's truth in that history. Recently a former theological student now engaged in the antipoverty program in an urban setting exclaimed, "Apathy! Its message is written in the language of hopelessness wherever I go." Apathy appears in many faces—despair, alienation, resentment, anomie, etc. Whatever its form, apathy is a burden of carewornness. It is also judgment, and an imperative to change for one who discerns the prophetic meaning of that burden.

Ministry as prophetic servanthood will be rooted in the organic relationship between historic existence and God's continuing intention to visit and redeem his people. From the perspective of ethics the primary mode of ministry is one of faithful and relevant action in the world. It is an entering into the labor of God as one who is willing to find his ministry en route. To find a ministry as opposed to applying an office involves risk. Such is the risk of the *Servus Servorum Dei*: one who is committed in faith to the notion that God's action in Christ is ever revealed anew in the

[34] See A. B. Davidson, "Prophets and Prophecy," *Hastings Dictionary of the Bible,* IV, 106-7.

living events of man's history. But ministry also requires relevancy. In the light of our exploration of the psychosocial matrix of human acts it is necessary to redirect the attention of pastoral care to the milieu and the wider social organizations that shape human behavior. In medical terms we must ask "Who is the patient?" As an agent of change the minister must recognize his responsibility as a sociotherapist as well as a psychotherapist.

However, the fulcrum for change in pastoral care remains rooted in the human capacity to respond to new self-images. Social and historical influences converge in the person who perceives himself as an actor (not a pawn) on the stage of history. Christ appears as man-come-of-age, as the New Being, who reveals the infinite depth of human possibility. Whether viewed phenomenologically as a Gestalt of grace or as the Christ of faith, this cognitive perception marks the beginning of change. Ministry as prophetic servanthood finds its task as a participant in this ongoing rediscovery of what it means to be a man. It is rooted in Christ's revelation of what it means to be a man for others.

The new context of pastoral care reflects the urgent need to recast professional ministry as the prophetic servant of an emerging lay ministry. New strategies of ministry whose flexible style provides a way of responding to the infinite variety of human need, individual and social, are called for. This does not diminish the need for an educated and skilled professional ministry, but it does mean more emphasis on the theologically reflective and adaptive functions of the pastoral office. In every age the church is faced with the perennial task of raising up an adequate ministry. This task must be fulfilled by men who are both indigenous and committed to the showing forth of God's truth.

Carl Wennerstrom was engaged in that task in his hospital

work and training. As a prophetic servant he pointed to an important step in that task, i.e., that ministers in training learn to accept their humanity in its weakness as well as in its strength as an indispensable resource in their work as *Servus Servorum Dei.* Kierkegaard's "knight of faith," I suggest, represents something of Carl Wennerstrom's passionate hope for ministry. It is the ministry of one who is "able to transform the leap into life into a normal gait, to be able to express perfectly the sublime in terms of the pedestrian." [35] This is the continuing miracle of ministry.

[35] Søren Kierkegaard, *Fear and Trembling,* trans. Robert Payne (New York: Oxford University Press, 1960), p. 48.

SOCIAL ETHICS AND PASTORAL CARE

James Luther Adams

Person and institution, law and liberty, individual and community are realities that are generally viewed as somehow standing in opposition to, or at least in tension with, each other. The same must be said of social ethics and psychotherapy, and also of social ethics and pastoral care. So much is the distance between them taken for granted that one seldom finds in the literature any substantial reference to their relationship, except to be sure that psychological and interpersonal aspects of social ethics receive consideration. But such discussions conspicuously ignore institutional questions.

The writer on Christian ethics usually does not concern himself with the social-ethical or institutional aspects of the conduct of pastoral care. On the other hand, the literature of pastoral care for its part largely ignores the problems presented by economic and political institutions, though to be sure the family as an institution, and perhaps also the school, receive attention. Then, too, one may encounter passing reference to economic institutions if the writer on psychotherapy or pastoral care comments on the inadequacy of the therapy of mere adjustment.

By way of justification for this virtual segregation, one could say that each discipline demands increasing specialization if it is to take seriously its own characteristic problems. This claim must be granted, but serious questions abide. Does not pastoral care relate to the prophetic aspect of the church's mission? Does not authentic therapy bring the restored person to participation in the normal institutional obligations of the churchman as citizen or of the church as a corporate body? Corresponding questions can be directed to the Christian (or secular) ethicist with respect to the impingement of pastoral care upon his discipline and its institutional concerns. These are among the searching questions that Carl Wennerstrom's dissertation poses. And certainly no one will claim that the answers are ready to hand.

It is Wennerstrom's thesis that social prophetism, bent on institutional reform, and a correspondingly rationalistic perspective on human personality, have promoted the neglect of pastoral care on the part of the liberal clergy; more than that, they tend to make the religious liberal shy away from the individual who has suffered personal catastrophe or is in some other way distressed in body, mind, or estate. Moreover, Wennerstrom views these lopsided emphases as contributing to an overdramatic conception of problem solving, and finally to a depersonalizing social distance between the pastoral counselor and the parishioner in distress. These impediments to authentic pastoral care Wennerstrom identifies under the names of rationalism, reformism, dramatics, and social distance. Moreover, he makes so bold as to speak of them as characteristic features of religious liberalism.

Wennerstrom's view of these dimensions of religious

liberalism, we should observe, is not simply a negative evaluation. Rather, he takes an ambivalent attitude. Indeed, as I read him, I find that he adopts a tragic view; religious liberalism has had noble intentions (he seems to say), but by reason of demonic lopsidedness it has engendered *hubris*. We might put it this way: the drive of liberalism has been to liberate the individual from authoritarianism and to open the way for autonomy and rationality. This drive has focused the energy of the liberal upon a militant reformism and rationalism, it has given him an overclear and overdramatic conception of his ability to solve problems, and it has reduced the desire or the capacity for intimate relationships. The liberal minister of this sort cannot "feel" or does not want to feel the other person as person, particularly if the other is in emotional distress.

Religious liberalism, in this view, has served as a sort of avalanche that has almost snowed under the liberal minister's capacity to perceive what does not fit into or support his highly selective, tailor-made thought structure. He maintains a social distance from the actual sufferer. Considering this outcome, Wennerstrom says of the major motifs of religious liberalism: Nothing fails like success. The situation is the more tragic insofar as the liberal minister, fired with reformism and rationalism, is unaware of this reality test. Pastoral care cannot become authentic until this kind of religious liberalism can be corrected. The correction will require an altered conception of man himself. In this connection John F. Hayward, in his chapter of this volume, looks beyond the stance of the minister and pungently sets forth the implications of Wennerstrom's outlook for a revision of the liberal-religious doctrine of man.

At first blush Wennerstrom's characterization of the ingredients of religious liberalism may appear to some readers to be merely a caricature. This impression of caricature could readily be gained from the elliptic summary I have given here. Actually, Wennerstrom's presentation exhibits more of the subtlety and paradox that attach to the reality.

We should observe immediately, however, that religious liberalism has no monopoly on the features Wennerstrom assigns to it. There are surprising similarities between religious liberalism and other religious movements of the modern period. For example, the first and the last features in Wennerstrom's list, rationalism and social distance, one could assign also to confessional orthodoxy as it has appeared since the seventeenth and eighteenth centuries. Indeed, even more of the four features are to be found in the Enlightenment. Both religious liberalism and confessional orthodoxy (with its rationalism in the formulation of "pure" doctrine) took on their special qualities during the period of the Enlightenment.

A more striking similarity than these, however, is to be remarked. In reading Wennerstrom's description of the features of religious liberalism one could readily substitute for religious liberalism the term "modern man," and the description would be almost equally cogent and pertinent. The four features adumbrated by Wennerstrom, when taken together, closely approximate what in many quarters have been summed up under the term "modernity." These four features, in one formulation or another, appear prominently in the typological writings of such analysts of modern man as Max Weber, Ernst Troeltsch, Paul Tillich, Karl Jaspers, Lewis Mumford, or Talcott Parsons. This observation of the similarity between Wennerstrom's description of the religious liberal and the regnant characterizations of modern man should not be at all surprising. Religious liberalism has taken its shape in part as an aspect of modernity. Indeed, this has been the proud claim of religious liberalism.

"Modern Man" as the Framework

What are the characteristic features of modernity? A comprehensive answer to this question would entail our comparing and contrasting "the modern" with "the medieval" and "the ancient." We need not enter here into such an elaborate analysis. It will suffice for our present purpose if we center attention directly upon what is meant by the terms "modern man" and "modernity."

At the outset we should observe that the concepts "modernity" and "modernization" possess a certain ambiguity. They can be viewed as connoting a value judgment; that is, they can be used as synonymous with good or desirable. At the same time they can express the intention to be merely descriptive. In either case, these concepts, like all concepts, are constructions. In this respect they necessarily select or emphasize certain features of the outlook or experience of modern man. Nuclear weapons, bacteriological warfare, fascism and communism, right-wing and left-wing movements, secularism and religious revivals, the social sciences and depth psychology, must be included among modern man's accomplishments or endeavors. One can readily see that there must be some discrepancy between modernity as a descriptive term and modernity as a term implying a positive value judgment.[1] From what has already been said about Wennerstrom's characterization of religious liberalism

---

[1] For a penetrating analysis of these ambiguities see Wilfred Cantwell Smith, *Modernisation of a Traditional Society* (New York: Asia Publishing House, 1965). See also Robert N. Bellah, ed., *Religion and Progress in Modern Asia* (New York: The Free Press, 1965). See especially the "epilogue" of the latter.

178

it becomes evident that he combines description and evaluation in his use of the term.

Let us now outline the framework within which we may consider our theme, Social Ethics and Pastoral Care among Liberals, toward the end of relating it to Wennerstrom's conception of pastoral care as it is conducted (or distorted) in the liberal churches.

It has been characteristic of modern man to rebel in the name of God or reason or freedom against authoritarianism, in the economic and political spheres as well as in the religious sphere. Similar religious motifs, or secularized versions of them, have played a central role also with respect to the idea of the person and with respect to conceptions of social organization. In turning away from authoritarianism the liberal has striven for the freedom and autonomy of the individual, for freedom of conscience, and freedom of choice. He has also made the claim to universality, bringing particular religious and cultural traditions under criticism. For example, he has claimed to discern and to represent a "natural religion" or a universal religiousness around the world. But especially has he believed that nature and history are amenable to human understanding and control, that man can be master of his fate, that reason, imagination, and will can give a new shape to human nature and the world. This world-shaping will has had its roots in the ethos of this-worldliness (as against otherworldliness). Moreover, old social ties of origin were to be dissolved. Pure and applied science have been viewed as allies in this venture. Religious liberalism, accordingly, attempted to end the warfare between religion and science.

All of these things were involved when modern man lost his confidence in merely traditional authorities. Thus he adopted what has been called substantial reason and techni-

179

cal reason, substantial in the sense of exercising freedom to consider and choose regarding the ends of life, and technical in the sense of seeking new means to achieve these ends. Everything was to be brought under the aegis of "one increasing purpose." This mentality, beginning with the Renaissance and especially with Francis Bacon, was supported and enhanced by the idea of progress, a dramatic interpretation of history which assumed both religious and secular formulation. What Wennerstrom calls rationalism gave rise also, then, to reformism. Modern man, with his faith in rationality, has believed that it is possible for him to define and solve problems anew if autonomy is allowed free rein. This whole process brought about a crisis in identity, not only because of the consequent acceleration of social change, but also because of the criticism directed at mere traditionalism in religion. This crisis in identity inevitably placed a heavy responsibility upon the psyche in face of a religious symbolism that was brought under question and also in face of a bewildering variety of emerging symbolism or reinterpreted symbolism.

We have spoken of individualism as an ingredient of liberalism. Strictly speaking, however, we may not say that liberalism is to be equated with atomistic individualism. Modern man has promoted the features of modernity we have mentioned by forming a multitude of associations, industrial, philanthropic, educational, professional, reformist, and religious. He has even created the modern state (in part a product of rational construction), an institution that did not exist in the Middle Ages. In the early modern period the state was assigned the function of protecting the rights of the individual, toward the end of liberating religious and economic institutions from political control.

In Anglo-American society, Calvinism and the common law, in collaboration, have given support here.

Of major significance was the proliferation of associations concerned with public policy (indispensable for the development of that uniquely modern phenomenon, public opinion) and of professional associations to promote rationality of skill and high standards of education and performance. The outcome of these associational efforts has been what we call the pluralistic society wherein freedom of choice is supposed to be given institutional configuration through freedom of association. At the same time modern man within and between these associations has attempted to promote freedom of individual thought and action. In large part this kind of society has been the product of rationalism and reformism, though of course with all sorts of residues from previous periods.

This whole movement in its Gestalt of concerns—freedom of conscience, individual responsibility, critique of traditional institutions and authorities, differentiation and independence of associations, cooperation between religion and science as well as mutual criticism, extension of the franchise, openness to social change—is something unique as well as fairly recent in history. This uniqueness becomes fully evident if one recalls that, in the main, historic religion, both West and East, has not favored pluralism, nor even the patterns of this-worldly change. Instead, it has promoted the authority of an elite that maintained a "divinely established," rigid pattern of society, and which inculcated the "virtue" of obedient humility. Only in the modern period has a dynamic conception of history become widely prevalent.

It is not accurate, therefore, to say that modernity in the West is the product of technology. Modernization has emerged from an internalized vision of history and responsibility which ventured to change history in order to bring man to his "maturity." Think, for example, of Immanuel Kant's conception of Enlightenment as the cutting of the apron strings of "minority." In the light of the worldview and the scope of this modernity one can scarcely accept Cyril Black's definition: "Modernization may be defined as the totality of the influence of the unprecedented increase in man's knowledge and control over his environment that has taken place in recent centuries." [2] This definition falls short of expressing the *ethos* of modernity, its vision of history, its boldness of innovation, its spirit of inquiry, its voluntarism of effort. At the same time, the definition does point to an important aspect of modernity, the technical rationalism and the relentless drive toward efficiency. This, too, was a goal of liberalism's "reformism," a reformism that eventually would itself require reform.

At this point we should observe a major psychological aspect of this whole development. One must be cautious about generalizations of this sort, particularly when they are applied to a whole period of historical development. Yet, it does seem plausible to say that, compared to the traditional medieval society, the modern rational, reforming, differentiating (pluralist) society draws much more upon the cognitive and voluntarist elements in the psyche than upon affective elements.[3] Likewise, the struggle of religious

[2] Quoted by Bellah, *Religion and Progress*, p. 170.

[3] One of the most suggestive treatments of these three aspects of the human psyche which I have encountered is by the Danish philosopher Harald Höffding, *Outlines of Psychology*, trans. Mary E. Lowndes (London: The Macmillan Co. 1892). It is a striking fact that this tripartite division into cognition, feeling, and will replaced in the eighteenth and nineteenth centuries the bipartite division into cognition and will which had been followed from the time of Aristotle. Rousseau

liberalism against traditionalist authoritarianism placed heavy demands upon the cognitive "faculties." In the modern period one does find, to be sure, certain conspicuous expressions of the affective side of personality. For example, the idea of romantic love did much to break through the old patterns that prevented courtship and marriage outside the boundaries of ascribed status. Moreover, in Protestant circles the conception of love set forth in the Gospels has been much stressed; but in the urbanized, competitive society this ethic of love has served in large measure as a compensatory ethic. To be sure, philanthropy, even highly organized philanthropy, has also been characteristic of modernity; but it gave expression more to cognition and will than to the affective (and affectional) faculties. It maintained its social distance. I shall not attempt in the present essay to pursue this motif about cognitive and affective faculties. Yet some aspects of modernity will become readily evident if we look at the evolution of liberalism, and especially if we look at its rationalism and reformism.

In the earlier modern period, rationalism and reformism gave rise to the economy of free enterprise. The means of production were geared to produce the maximum amount of goods at the maximum rate of speed and at the minimum cost. These goods were delivered to a free and anonymous authority, the market, a mechanism that was to promote competition and efficiency, and which in turn was supposed to issue in an automatic, ecological balance or harmony. Likewise, the innovation and testing of ideas were to be

and Kant exercised decisive influence here. My attribution of cognitive and voluntarist qualities to liberalism does not come from Höffding. William Dilthey, it will be recalled, formulated his typology of world views in terms of the tripartite psychology, discerning respectively three major world views, those oriented to reason, to will, and to feeling.

promoted by "free trade in ideas." Efficiency became a moral demand, a demand that was not previously made by Christianity. By the nineteenth century the ideal of efficiency had become practically a religious demand.

In order to initiate these changes a vigorous social reform had to be carried through, particularly for the sake of freeing business and the church from the restrictions of special privilege or of political control. This reform has been characterized by Henry Maine as the movement from status to contract. Under the aegis of these demands all sorts of new organizations came to birth. Insofar as these organizations were "instrumental" associations they continued vigorously to promote rationality and efficiency. Indeed, these values seem to have taken precedence over concern for the individual person as such. Impersonality was required if the free trade in goods and ideas was to be effective.

Here we see a striking paradox: the requirements of impersonality in the social system and the need for aggressive personality in the personality system if the social system was to be effective in reaching its goals. The Friends in their history combined these elements, on the one hand (for example), demanding that price tags take the place of dickering, and on the other hand setting a high value on the I-Thou relation, yet moving steadily from the meetinghouse to the countinghouse. But the emphasis on personhood and individualism was largely a class phenomenon; it brought the middle class onto the stage of history, but at the same time it moved the lower classes into a more depressed style of living than was characteristic of the earlier period. Social distance was by no means diminished, either between the old aristocracy and the new bourgeoisie or between the middle and the lower classes, or even within the middle class. Moreover, freedom rather than justice was the dominant ideal. Justice was to be taken care of by means of the automatic harmony.

Rationality and reformism in time, however, found themselves confronted by new demands. Laissez-faire came into crisis. The old liberalism was not able, after all, to enter into the promised land of automatic harmony. Instead, structural maladjustment became the disorder of the day, imbalance between production and consumption, cyclical unemployment. Millions of people became victims of the automatic disharmony. Presently, a new liberalism appeared on the horizon, demanding that private rights be qualified by communal responsibilities and that the community as a whole assume responsibility to achieve greater economic stability. Consequently, a more positive conception of the state came to birth. The new situation demanded a revision of the old ideas of rationality and reform, precisely in order to protect or elevate some of the people who had been forgotten. In short, rationality and efficiency were required to bring the welfare state into being (and religious liberalism played a positive as well as a negative role here). At the same time they did not alter the ethos of social distance.

The sense of success, however, was short-lived. Within the period of a generation this new ordering of institutions in its turn brought new frustrations. The people who were to be recovered for the enjoyment of the benefits of the welfare state now protested against the status of dependency induced by the system. The demand of historic liberalism expresses itself here, the demand for autonomy. The recipients of the welfare would prefer to be given employment rather than largesse, and also to have some share in the enjoyment of self-determination.[4]

[4] James Luther Adams, "Exiles Trapped in the Welfare State," *The Unitarian Christian* 22 (Winter, 1967), 3-9.

In this situation the Black Power Movement has intensified the demands and the tensions; and its leaders have accused the liberals of being both ineffectual and hypocritical. During the past forty or fifty years, we should add, the tensions have been augmented by the world-embracing ideological and international conflicts between capitalism, socialism, fascism, and communism. Meanwhile, the churches have been compelled to reassess their own self-image and their mission. Taken together, these tensions and demands have induced in wide circles a whole series of identity crises. Indeed, they have given rise to the very concept of identity crisis.

It is no accident that during the past two generations psychotherapy and pastoral counseling have taken on a new significance. Indeed, it was during this period that they acquired the status of special disciplines, partly as a consequence of the tremendous stimulus provided by advances in the study of psychology and especially of depth psychology. As Seward Hiltner shows in his chapter in the present volume, the religious liberals have provided much of the significant leadership in the development of the new discipline of pastoral psychology. From Wennerstrom's point of view, however, the *hubris* of the old religious liberalism has by no means played itself out. Moreover, the social-distance characteristic of the liberal-religious mentality continues to function as an impediment to the effective practice of pastoral counseling among religious liberals.

We have now traced in barest outline the morphology of liberalism adumbrated by Wennerstrom when he speaks of rationalism, reformism, dramatics, and social distance. From this survey it should become clear that Wennerstrom's description and critique of religious liberalism, if it is understood in historical context, is actually a description

186

and criticism of much that goes under the name modernity. But even as an outline the account is a truncated one. There is more to the story.

Tension as Modernity Emerged

Did not eighteenth-century liberalism attempt to correct the distortions of the human psyche brought about by rationalism? Did not the Enlightenment itself turn against rationalism by stressing the role of benevolence, sympathy, feeling, and the like? And did not Romanticism also turn against the rationalism of the Enlightenment by extolling spontaneity of feeling, and also by stressing the preciousness and integrity of the individual, and even by appealing to a mystical sense of transcendence, the sense of the brooding presence of the Whole, or of the Infinite, in every part? Did not these movements attempt to correct the overemphasis upon the cognitive and voluntarist elements in human nature by appealing to something deeper and more fraternal or affectional in man? And did not the evangelical Awakenings profoundly alter the Anglo-American religious mentality?

It is true that from Romanticism an organic, neo-medieval social theory did emerge which promoted a Catholic revival, but there is little evidence to show that either the eighteenth-century benevolence theory or Romanticism gave new impetus or content to pastoral care. Nor did the evangelistic revivals significantly correct the element of social distance in interpersonal relations. The Great Awakening of the eighteenth century called the individual out of his loneliness and into the enjoyment of a seemingly total commitment of heart and soul. Also the Methodist class-meeting developed a certain intimacy of personal relations, but it developed rigid moralistic tests of the authenticity of conversion.

Adam Smith pointed out that revivalism brought the lonely and forgotten man out of isolation and gave him a new dignity by convincing him that he had an eternal soul worth saving, but that he soon found himself caught in a vise of moralistic conformity. At the outset, then, this revivalism made appeal against rationalism in favor of affective elements, but in the end impersonal and cognitive and voluntarist elements prevailed. The individuality of the person was submerged by means of a concocted identity forced on the convert by social coercion.

The Second Awakening of the early decades of the nineteenth century was likewise a turn away from rationalism (the emphasis on clarity of cognition), but increasingly it took on a communal and even nationalistic character. It aimed to regenerate "communities en bloc," and in the end it sought to justify itself in face of criticism at the hands of the religious liberals by claiming to contribute to national health and religious self-identity, in short, to patriotism. In connection with this thrust the revivals brought into play a kind of technological rationalism. In 1835 Charles Finney argued that the forces that were "unfriendly to religion" appealed to "the great political and other worldly excitements," and that the cause of religion was to be promoted only through "the counterexcitements," "the religious excitements," of revivalism. Finney in this vein spelled out the techniques for saving souls.[5]

In some measure the revivalism of the nineteenth and

[5] For this analysis and evaluation of the revivalism of the early nineteenth century and its contribution to a sense of national destiny see Perry Miller, *The Life of the Mind in America* (New York: Harcourt, Brace & World, 1965), especially chapter 1.

the early twentieth centuries in America can be viewed also as an evasive and atavistic reaction to threatening social change or maladjustment. Instead of attacking the new social problems of the receding frontier through rational analysis and reformism, it offered (somewhat in the manner of Billy Graham today) the deceptive remedy of individual "regeneration" and of return to "the good old ways" of conventional moralism in the private sphere. On the whole, though not entirely, revivalism has been the haven of political conservatism, and it has been hostile to reformism. Even if one holds that revivalism was the soil out of which social reform was to grow, nevertheless one cannot argue that it overcame the social distance of which Wennerstrom speaks. It did not promote concern for the pastoral care of individual souls; through the stereotyping of the conversion experience it tended to treat them all alike, as brands to be snatched from the burning.

In the nineteenth century a more personal approach is to be observed among the religious liberals who criticized and opposed the revivals. Characteristic for this tradition are the views of Henry Ware, Jr., professor of pulpit eloquence and pastoral care at Harvard Divinity School in the 1830's and 1840's, and formerly minister of the Second Church in Boston. It is significant that Ware was conscious of the tension between the prophetic role and the pastoral role of the minister. Indeed, he warned against reformism as prone to underestimate the importance and uniqueness of the pastoral role, and especially to militate against the personal quality required for that role. "We are too ready," he says, "to regard Christianity as designed to operate on society, and accomplish a great work for the progress and information of the world." Even if we look at a single parish, he continues, "we are too apt to see it in this general view,

189

and address it as a community, rather than as a collection of individuals." [6]

It would be difficult to find in the nineteenth century in America a more painstaking elaboration of the nature of the pastoral office than that of Ware. The flavor of his conception can be indicated by two or three quotations. Speaking of the concern of the true pastor for the individual member of the flock, he asserts:

The man who is familiar with the situation, trials and wants of those whom he addresses; who goes up to the pulpit from their firesides and chambers—full of interest in their characters, and sympathy with their condition—feels that he is not meeting a congregation in the abstract but men and women whom he knows and cares for, and who are waiting to catch from him something which will suit their necessities, and be for them guidance and improvement.[7]

The preacher's lack of close personal association with members of his flock, according to Ware, is the principal source of the spurious, inflated rhetoric of the pulpit:

I know no cure for false rhetoric like this. And whenever I witness the grandiloquence of the sophomore in the pulpit,— when I hear there the flashy commonplaces of flowers, and rivers, and clouds, and rainbows, and dews—when I listen to the empty music of periods which are rounded only to be harmonious, and the tricks of speech which perform no office for the sense; then I say that all this miserable foppery—as false to good taste as it is to the souls of men and the truth

[6] Henry Ware, Jr., *The Connexion Between the Duties of the Pulpit and the Pastoral Office: An Introductory Address Delivered to the Members of the Theological School in Cambridge, October 18 and 25, 1830* (Cambridge: Williams and Brown, 1830), p. 7.
[7] *Ibid.,* p. 9.

of God—could never have been committed by a man who walked faithfully among his people, caring for their actual wants, and anxious to feed them with knowledge and understanding.[8]

Ware is so convinced of the indispensability of the personal relation between the pastor and the parishioner that he frowns upon the clerical practice of exchanging pulpits: "However sleepers may be sometimes most effectually awakened by the warning cry of a stranger, the whole flock is best watched and fed by regular and stated shepherds." [9]

It will be noted in these passages, however, that Ware stresses "knowledge and understanding" (cognitive awareness) as the contribution of the pastor. It is possible that Ware in his practice as a pastoral counselor amply exhibited the affective as well as the cognitive quality, in short, that his practice was better than his theory. In the main, however, his theory apparently conformed to the tradition within Protestantism which was moralistic and was lacking in the empathy and sympathy that Wennerstrom desiderates.

Modern Development of the Professions

Now, from what source did Carl Wennerstrom get this criterion of the authentic stance of the pastoral counselor? Clearly, it did not originate in merely individual hunch or insight. Actually, the criterion was the outcome of a kind of rationalism, a cognition, which has been promoted in recent years by professional students on the basis of empirical observation of pastoral counseling. Seward Hiltner in one of his essays has given an account of these developments (up to 1951) in the dialogue between pastoral

[8] *Ibid.*, p. 13.
[9] *Ibid.*, p. 19.

theology and secular psychology.[10] So far from promoting social distance in pastoral care and in psychotherapy this analytical or rational empiricism has actually made us aware of the nature of social distance and of the impediment it can create for the pastoral counselor.[11]

Here we should observe a highly significant aspect of the relation between pastoral psychology and psychotherapy, namely, the development of a professional outlook or mentality. This observation has so many ramifications for the theme of the present chapter that I must dwell at some length on the nature and implications of this professional outlook.

It must be granted that professionalism can become the occasion for the frustration of the work of the pastoral counselor, for example, by inducing him to consider the parishioner who is in distress as a "case." In all of the professions the disease of professionalism appears especially in the rigidities that belong to orthodoxy or to bureaucratization. But the professional attitude of course should not be

[10] Seward Hiltner, "Pastoral Theology and Psychology," in Arnold S. Nash, ed., *Protestant Thought in the Twentieth Century* (New York: The Macmillan Co., 1951), pp. 181-98.

[11] One of the earliest definitions of "social distance" appears in the article by the Chicago sociologist Robert E. Park, entitled "The Concept of Social Distance," *Journal of Applied Sociology* VIII (July-August, 1924), 339-344. Here he contrasts the "impulse that leads us to enter imaginatively into the other persons' minds, to share their experience and sympathize with their pains and pleasures, joys and sorrows, hopes and fears," with the sense of social distance which bespeaks self-consciousness and reserve and which appears in such group phenomena as race consciousness or class consciousness. Emory S. Bogardus during the same decade (and later) wrote extensively on the concept, and contrived devices for the measurement of social distance. Sociometry later on developed similarly precise means for measuring social distance. The concept of social distance appears frequently in the literature of race relations and of pastoral psychology.

equated with professionalism in these senses. Indeed, the authentic professional attitude recognizes these and other dangers of professionalism.

The concept of the professions is by no means a strictly modern one, though it has been developed in elaborate ways in the modern period. It can be traced back to antiquity, particularly in the practice of law and medicine. Moreover, already by the second century the Christian churches began (under pagan influence) to consider the work of the priest as in part a professional task: the idea became current that it is not enough for the man of God to know the tradition—the sacred literature, the liturgy, the administration of the sacraments. It was held that he should study rhetoric in order to become familiar with the literature of the humanities and also in order to become a proficient teacher and preacher. (Augustine tells us that he was first attracted to Christianity by the "rhetorical" skill of Bishop Ambrose, rhetorical in the broad cultural sense just indicated.) Eventually, the preparation of the minister came to require systematic theological education with its various disciplines. Even the care of souls acquired a certain professional quality, for example, in the systematic study of cases of conscience. Here one should mention also the venerable tradition of "spiritual direction." The spiritual director became a highly specialized figure. Indeed, in the Roman Catholic Church a variety of "schools" of spiritual direction developed. Previous to this, however, the medieval universities exercised a decisive influence in the shaping of the disciplines of the professions. As Whitehead (*Adventures of Ideas*) and other historians have observed, the development of the definition and the ideals of the professions represents one of the major elements in the history of modernity in the West.

During the past generation or two both psychotherapy

and pastoral counseling in differing degrees have taken on a professional character. What is meant by the term *profession* in this context? A professional man is one who possesses a higher education in the humanities and the sciences: he has been exposed to the disciplines that familiarize him with the characteristic values of the cultural tradition; he has the task of criticizing, transmitting, and applying these value preferences; he understands and improves his special skills in terms of a rational theory; he acquires his skills and his theory in relation to the disciplines of the university; and, generally, he belongs to a professional association that articulates a consensus with respect to professional ethics and with respect to the standards of the performance of his skills.[12]

This list of criteria is not exhaustive; nor is it once-for-all "established." Indeed, in a rapidly changing society with rapidly expanding knowledge considerable disagreement develops in face of the claims of newly emerging professions. We should add here that the clergyman is not to be brought completely under the rubric of the professions. He stands also in the tradition of a religious community, a community of faith. Moreover, some of his skills, for example, the skill of pastoral counseling, may be viewed as quasi-professional.

In the area of pastoral care the past generation has witnessed the appearance of professional associations and of learned journals concerned not only with pastoral counseling but also with psychotherapy. Seward Hiltner in his chapter in the present volume has outlined the development of pastoral counseling as a discipline, contributed to in primary ways, though not exclusively, by religious liberals.

[12] James Luther Adams, "The Social Import of the Professions," *American Association of Theological Schools Bulletin* 23 (June, 1958), 152-68.

This whole development is an aspect of the rationality that attaches to modernity. Moreover, the advance of the discipline of training in pastoral counseling has required a vigorous reformism in the ministry, in theological education, and in the relation between theology and the behavioral sciences, areas in which much unfinished business remains to be undertaken. One consequence of these developments has been the appearance of a new awareness of ethical dimensions of pastoral counseling which were previously of simpler perception, particularly with regard to guilt, anxiety, autonomy, conscience, and identity. A whole range of new conceptualization has been the result. The appearance of this new discipline has had considerable effect in turn upon the study of the older disciplines of theology and ethics; and it has uncovered psychological and sociological dimensions of religion which were previously much less appreciated.

The "professional" element in this development is to be seen also in the awareness of the limitations of the pastoral counselor. Even the least instructed minister today recognizes that ours is a world of professionals. Indeed, even the man who considers himself omnicompetent by reason of his ordination as "a man of God" is aware of his responsibility to recognize his limitations by knowing when he should refer the troubled person to a specialist. On the other hand, the better instructed pastor will be aware also of the existence of various "schools" or types of psychotherapy.

The perceptive minister in face of the variety of these types will also be aware of the conflicting "images of man" presented by these types, images that bespeak rival philosophical or theological conceptions of man. Almost at random I select an example here, the shift in Freud's thinking from his earlier to his later period, a shift, according to

Erik Erikson, from an epicurean to a stoic conception.[13] We should mention here also the profound change in the conception of human nature which has resulted from the adoption of the theory of the unconscious.

Pastoral Care and Personal Ethics

These changes and variations have shed new light on the problems of personal ethics. New implications of historic theological-ethical doctrines have thus been disclosed. For example, the pastoral counselor who is a religious liberal seeks new formulation of the old doctrine of autonomy. He sees it to be his ethical responsibility not to try to *impose* an ethical standard but rather to enable the parishioner to achieve freedom of choice; at the same time he acknowledges that he must try to assist him to overcome obsession with self. Wennerstrom, to his credit, recognized that in this whole area of personal ethics special problems appear because of the inadequacy of the ingredients of religious liberalism. For example, the parishioner will very likely need to overcome the rationalism that looks for a clear and definitive solution to his problem; he may need to be content with something less than a dramatic solution. Indeed, something other than a merely ethical issue may be at stake; the question of facing tragedy and of going "beyond tragedy." (Here the pastoral counselor is confronted by theological problems that the secular psychotherapist may evade.) The same thing must be said regarding problems of conscience, of guilt, and anxiety. The advantage enjoyed by both the counselor and the parishioner is not only their common membership in a religious community but also the sense of

[13] Erik H. Erikson, *Young Man Luther* (New York: W. W. Norton and Co., 1958), p. 253.

the availability of more than human resources. In our day, however, when old symbols have lost much of their meaning, the task of the counselor is profoundly difficult. Again, a professional skill is almost required not only to venture new formulations but also to do so in face of a particular individual who possesses his own special semantic habits and frustrations.

One other professional aspect of the work of the counselor should be mentioned here. We can say that Carl Wennerstrom's critical characterization of the ingredients of religious liberalism in relation to pastoral care is itself a manifestation of professional analysis. He made the analysis in his pursuit of the professional, doctoral degree, and toward the end of improving the theory and practice of pastoral counseling. The conceptual apparatus that he employs he adapted from social psychology and psychotherapy. Moreover, his view that the pastoral counselor, instead of resorting to rationalism, should overcome social distance and "feel with" the person in distress, is a view that is characteristic of the emphasis of certain schools of psychotherapy. In this connection he would have recognized that the parishioner who seeks pastoral counsel wants more than sympathy and empathy. Not everyone can give him the empathy he cherishes. The pastoral counselor who offers sympathy or empathy, the parishioner knows, is something more than a mere sympathizer or empathizer. He is expected to offer counsel on the basis of experience and reflection in these matters, and toward the end of therapy or healing. Here again rationality plays a significant role. Indeed, a modicum of social distance or detachment will be required if the therapy is to achieve its purpose. Talcott Parsons speaks of this sort of detachment as "affective neutrality."

197

I have spoken only briefly and in general terms of the concern of the pastoral counselor for personal ethics. This concern generally, and for obvious reasons, takes priority. A major problem appears in the struggle against regressive, constrictive forms of moral control. The concern for personal ethics cannot be separated from reflection upon the basic issues of life and tragedy and death—the meaning of life itself, the meaning also of forgiveness and reconciliation and fellowship. Here the counselor and the parishioner are led to the boundary situation where one becomes newly aware of the ultimate resources upon which man depends and in which he places his trust. Carl Wennerstrom in this connection speaks of the presence of the Holy Spirit, thus pointing to a reality that transcends both the counselor and the parishioner.

It must be recognized that typical pastoral counseling (and also the training for pastoral counseling) gives major attention to personal ethics. But the matter cannot be left here. The work of the counselor is not the only task of the minister. He is a teacher, a preacher, an executive director, a man in the community. None of these roles can be divorced from his task as pastoral counselor. In all of these roles the openness, the sympathy, the tragic sense of life must inform his activity. At the same time the social-ethical demands upon the church as a corporate body and upon the individual member make their claims; and these claims impinge upon the work of the counselor.

Objective and Subjective Value

How, then, are we to conceive of the relation between pastoral counseling and these social-ethical demands? This question brings us to recognize a curious anomaly. For the sake of healing, the counselor is constrained to give at least initial priority to the personal problems of the troubled person. Yet, these personal problems cannot be resolved apart from the context of the corporate responsibilities of the church and the individual with respect to social and institutional problems. Every personal problem is a social problem, and every social problem is a personal problem. Wennerstrom's presentation of social action (reformism) in contrast to pastoral care could make it appear that social-ethical problems and demands—and particularly institutional aspects of social change—must be put on the side for the sake of the intimate personal relation that is requisite for authentic counseling. But I doubt that in the last analysis Wennerstrom would accept this interpretation.

In this connection it is pertinent to recall a distinction that has been given currency by Ernst Troeltsch, the distinction between subjective and objective values.[14] This distinction has to do with the difference between the values that attach to private life and those that belong to the public order. The subjective values spring entirely from the individual's relation as an individual to God, his direct relation to other persons, and his internal dialogue in the striving for integrity. Here truthfulness, honesty in self-awareness, thoughtfulness, openness, benevolence, and loyalty are the characteristic values. The objective values, on the other hand, are the ethical claims that inform or guide men in the realm of "history"—the sphere of group life which demands institutional expression. Objective values require in-

[14] Ernst Troeltsch, "Fundamental Problems of Ethics," the translation of a portion of which appears in Warren F. Groff and Donald E. Miller, *The Shaping of Modern Christian Thought*, trans. Donald E. Miller (Cleveland: World Publishing Company, 1968), pp. 23-35. See also Friedrich von Hügel, *Essays and Addresses*, First Series (London: J. M. Dent, 1929), pp. 153-54.

stitutional participation for their manifestation. They attach to the structures of society, the family (especially in its relation to other spheres), the state, the community, property and production, education, science, art, and "organized" religion. The moral life, than, comprises both subjective and objective values, in each case individual and social. It is not appropriate to interpret the distinction in such a way as to make it cognate with that between inner and outer or between interiorization and institutionalization. Nor is it appropriate to promote a dualism between subjective and objective values. Each ultimately requires the other.

Now, it is understandable (as we have said) if psychotherapy and pastoral counseling give primary, if not exclusive, attention to subjective values. The difficulties of the troubled individual present themselves for the most part as interpersonal. They do not ordinarily arise out of conflicts or frustrations the individual has encountered as a consequence of his attempting to change institutions. Moreover, the therapeutic process promoted by the counselor cannot take place directly in the context of the larger institutional structures. It appears, at least initially, in the I-Thou encounter between the counselor and the parishioner, or in a small group, or in the family. This factor, the ostensibly interpersonal character of both the problem and the therapy, has the effect of drawing attention to subjective rather than to objective values.

The concentration of attention upon subjective values tends to appear also in the preaching of the minister who deals with personal problems he encounters directly in the parish. The minister who allows the strictly interpersonal problems encountered in his work as counselor to determine his preaching will tend to select sermon topics such as "How to Overcome Your Worries," or "The War Between the Generations," or "Peace of Mind," or "Peace of Soul," or "What We Must Learn from Freud." He will seldom choose controversial topics regarding public policy.

The reference here to Freud possesses a special pertinence. In the main, Freud's experience was that of the clinical worker and not of the citizen concerned with public policy; in this clinical concern he dealt with the disturbed state of the individual and not with any systematic analysis of institutional problems. Moreover, when he concerned himself with the problems of "civilization and its discontents" he did so through a psychological approach which interpreted the major problem of civilization as that of the coercion of the individual and the major problem of the individual as that of the renunciation (or sublimation) of instinct. Equally important is the fact that he attempted to understand the fundamental facts and problems of human nature in terms of inner-family relationships. Thus his basic conceptual apparatus was drawn in part from the observation of the individual (repression, anxiety, projection), and in part from the observation of the family. Insofar as his basic concepts were oriented to the family his vocabulary was domestic; it presupposed a familial model, providing a paradigm of family relationships—between child and mother, child and father, child and siblings. Domestic metaphors rather than political dominate in his writings, and subjective values rather than objective. His major tendency was to subordinate cultural and broadly sociological and political factors to biological and psychological factors, that is, to the private man. His contributions to understanding and to therapy should not be minimized. Yet, his neglect of sociology and the other social sciences continues to be evident in his influence, despite the efforts of Karen Horney, Harry Stack Sullivan, Erich Fromm, and others. Freud supplied a sanction for indifference to politics. Moreover, he viewed the state as mainly an engine for the protection of society against anarchy. In this respect his outlook is much more similar to that of Lutheranism and erotic Jewish mysticism than to that of the Jewish tradition where the positive demand for social righteousness informs the life of a covenanted people.

A similar restriction of interest and perception is to be observed in the psychology of religion as generally conceived. We may take William James as an example here. In *The Varieties of Religious Experience* one finds almost exclusive presentation of the individual in his relation to subjective values. Conversion, the once-born and the twice-born man, the reorientation of values, are not dealt with in the context of institutional behavior, but rather as inner-personal and interpersonal phenomena. James's interpretation of pragmatism led him to look for the influence of religion as almost entirely in the personal sphere. "By their fruits ye shall know them" was in the main interpreted in terms of personal ethics and not in terms of institutional analysis or consequences.

Max Weber states that "James's pragmatic valuation of the significance of religious ideas according to their influence on life is . . . a true child of the world of ideas of the Puritan home of that eminent scholar." [15] This characterization can be quite misleading if it is taken to mean that James's perception of the pragmatic meaning of Christian conversion

[15] Max Weber, *The Protestant Ethic and the Spirit of Capitalism*, trans. Talcott Parsons (Paperback ed.; New York: Charles Scribner's Sons, 1958), pp. 232-33. For a critique of Weber's presentation of Puritanism and his distorted conception of "the Protestant ethic" see James L. Adams, "Theokratie, Kapitalismus und Demokratie," *Zeitschrift für Evangelishe Ethik* 12 (July-September, 1968), pp. 247-67.

was a Puritan perception. Puritanism, and the Calvinism in which it was rooted, strove not only to engender the twice-born man, but also to promote a new order of society. Its characteristic metaphors are not psychological or domestic but political (for example, covenant and kingdom of God). It promoted social as well as individual salvation. In line with its doctrine of sanctification Puritanism threw much of its energy into forming associations that provided not only a social discipline but also a means of reforming society. William James was personally "unmusical" in this area of the practical import of religion (and of Calvinism), as is to be observed not only in *The Varieties* . . . but also in his own life-style. When, for example, Francis Greenwood Peabody urged James to join him and other Harvard colleagues in an attempt to influence the Massachusetts legislature, James in effect replied, "Leave me out of that sort of thing." He was much more interested in the psychology of the individual than in institutional behavior, in subjective than in objective values. In his presentation the prophetic dimension of religion was reduced to the vanishing point. In this respect he was more similar to the pietist than to the Puritan. In short, the diversity of experience presented in his work is so limited that the title *The Varieties of Religious Experience* is scarcely justified.

This limitation of interest and perception on the part of William James has often been observed by the sociologists. It has been sharply criticized also by Roman Catholics. Recently I have encountered a typical Roman Catholic criticism that is worth mentioning here. In going through a volume from William James's private library, now in Widener Library at Harvard, I found a handwritten letter of May 10, 1909, from Baron Friedrich von Hügel to James, commenting on the latter's *Varieties* (which James had sent to him). After expressing grateful indebtedness to James in this letter, von Hügel goes on to speak of his "dissatisfactions." "I continue to feel," he says, that "your taking of the religious experience as separable from its institutional, historical occasions and environment. . .to be schematic, a priori, not what your method, so concrete and a posteriori, seems to demand." Von Hügel concludes by saying that if James in *The Varieties* had presented this broader, institutional dimension of religion, "The result, I think, would have been of greater permanent value and instructiveness."

In response to this criticism James might have repeated what he says in his first lecture on *The Varieties*, that his standpoint was that of psychology, "the only branch of learning in which I am particularly versed." Moreover, he could point to an emphasis in his interpretation of religion which is of primary significance to the pastoral counselor as Wennestrom presents him:

The recesses of feeling, the darker, blinder strata of character, are the only places in the world in which we catch real fact in the making, and directly perceive events happen, and how work is actually done. Compared with this world of individualized feelings, the world of generalized objects which the intellect contemplates is without solidity or life. As in stereoscopic or kinoscopic pictures seen outside the instrument, the third dimension, the movement, the vital element, are not there.[16]

In this vein James speaks eloquently to the pastoral counselor when he says that to attempt to describe the world while leaving out "the various feelings of the individual

[16] William James, *The Varieties of Religious Experience* (New York: Longmans, Green, 1902), pp. 501-2.

pinch of destiny, all the various spiritual attitudes," is to leave the world a hollow and abstract affair. "What keeps religion going," he says, "is something else than abstract definitions and systems of concatenated adjectives, and something different from faculties of theology and their professors." [17]

James's emphasis upon the "feelings of the individual pinch of destiny" brings him into close affinity with the existentialists. Here again the primary concern is with the subjective values. Kierkegaard has exercised a decisive influence on both theological and secular writers among the existentialists, for example, Bultmann and Heidegger. He was so passionately concerned with subjective values and *Innerlichkeit* that his concern for objective values found expression only in his criticism of the bourgeois church and of the mass society. He showed little interest in a positive doctrine of the church or of society. His type of pietism helped to create the vacuum into which Marxism rushed with resentful fervor. Kierkegaard himself preferred old-fashioned monarchy to stave off mobocracy.

In general, however, pietism and Marxism exhibit opposite forms of lopsidedness, the former being concerned with subjective and the latter with objective values. One is reminded of Sainte Beuve's word that nothing is so much like a swelling as a hole. In view of the fact that Freud's restriction of perception is formally analogous to that of existentialism it is understandable that Erich Fromm has attempted to persuade the Freudians to study Marx, and the Marxists to study Freud. Fromm, to be sure, prefers the ideas of the young Marx before Marx became a Marxist.

[17] *Ibid.*, p. 447.

205

The existentialist ethic represents an individualist bias; the individual is admonished to liberate himself from the routinized, banal, and technologized society toward the end of achieving a new responsibility; but the conception of responsibility does not carry with it a positive institutional articulation.

We have noted the similarity between pietism and existentialism, particularly in the primary concern for subjective values. It should be added, however, that pietism sometimes promotes the concern for objective values in the sense that it favors philanthropic endeavor that aims to ameliorate social evils. This social outreach of pietism, however, does not go so far as to include social-structural analysis or basic institutional transformation. Conversion is for individuals; according to the gospel of Billy Graham, institutions will change if the individuals are "converted." Here one should observe the contrast with prophetism of the sort stemming from the Old Testament which exhibits concern for both objective and subjective values. We think here of Isaiah, Jeremiah, and the Psalms, or of the Puritans and the Friends.

The contrast between the emphasis on subjective and the emphasis on objective values is to be seen in the contrast between Lutheranism and Calvinism. The Lutherans have tended, on the basis of their interpretation of the New Testament, to emphasize *Innerlichkeit* and the world of subjective values as the salient sphere of religion, and to leave the world of objective values (beyond the realm of the family) to the magistrates under God. This division of labor into the Two Kingdoms assigns to the individual the vocation of doing his own thing in private life and the obligation of obedience to the magistrates in the public sphere. Hence,

206

the vocation of citizenship was alien to Luther.[18] (In contemporary Lutheranism this conception of the two kingdoms has been considerably revised.)

The Calvinist, on the other hand, emphasized a general as well as a specialized conception of vocation, the general responsibility to work for the establishment of a community of justice as well as the more specialized responsibility to perform one's own daily work. Out of the performance of the generalized vocation the Puritans and their descendants formed the many associations to which reference has been made earlier. Max Weber's conception of "the Protestant ethic" completely ignores this generalized conception of vocation (which stems from theocratic Calvinism and which, we should add, often issues in a conspiratorial conception of history as a struggle between the righteous and the damned, the saints and the sinners). He excludes from the record the reformist associations that struggled to correct what he calls the Protestant ethic. Weber does, to be sure, note the legalist mentality of Calvinism which stands in contrast with the Lutheran mentality. Some of these con-

[18] The lopsidedness in Lutheranism with respect to the emphasis on subjective values and the doctrine of vocation has militated in the public order in Germany against the Lutherans' coming to terms positively and creatively with the reformist element in modernity. Hans Kohn has recently pointed out the detrimental consequences for Germany. "Fascism," he says, "was the 'philosophy' of politically and socially retarded nations faced by the challenge of modernity. . . . There is today no grass-roots democracy, as there was none in Weimar; there is only a party hierarchy and a bureaucracy planning in secrecy behind a parliamentary spirit, or perhaps any spirit. . . . A world of 'highly individual values has emerged, which puts the experienced happiness of the individual in first place and increasingly lets the so-called whole slip from sight.' . . . human values are mostly those of the private individual." Review of *The Future of Germany* by Karl Jaspers and of *Society and Democracy in Germany* by Ralf Dahrendorf, in *Psychiatry and Social Science Review* II (June, 1968), 22-23.

trasts between Calvinism and Lutheranism appear in the differences between the corresponding conceptions of pastoral care. We shall presently return to this theme.

But first we should note a striking similarity that obtains between the various outlooks that stress subjective rather than objective values. We have seen that Freudianism, James's interpretation of religion, existentialism, pietism, and revivalism turn out to belong to the same family. Strange bedfellows! Freud, James, Kierkegaard, Bultmann, and Billy Graham!

Sociology and Pastoral Care

The question now arises: Does pastoral care belong to this family? This is a crucial question for the consideration of the relations between pastoral care and social or institutional ethics. It would seem that it does belong to this family if its concern is mainly with subjective values.

Our question then becomes: Can pastoral care be equated with pastoral psychology? That is, can pastoral psychology get along without pastoral sociology? Can psychotherapy get along without sociotherapy? These are questions that have been coming increasingly to the fore during the past decade, though it must be remembered that already thirty years ago social scientists attempted (with little success) to raise these issues. These questions imply the necessity of examining the training of the psychotherapist and the pastoral counselor. In some theological schools the proportion of the number of staff members and courses in the area of pastoral care is much larger than that in social ethics, sociology, and sociotherapy. Moreover, clinical training is widely interpreted in such a way as largely to exclude clinical training in community organization and in agencies concerned with public policy.

Wennerstrom's unfinished dissertation does not explicitly deal with these questions. He appears mainly to say that certain features of religious liberalism, which we have seen to be the features also of modernity, militate against the conduct of authentic pastoral care. But his solution was not to liquidate modernity. Instead, he wished to protect pas· toral care from the ravages of a demonic modernity.

Obviously, the limitations of space here do not permit our dealing with these questions in an adequate way. We must confine our discussion to two major aspects of the subject: first, the role of sociology in the understanding of pastoral care (and mental health), specifically with respect to social ethics; and, second, the place of objective values in the practice of pastoral care.

At this late date it is not necessary to belabor the claim that the pastoral counselor (and the psychotherapist) requires the assistance of the social sciences if he is to achieve self-understanding with regard to his role. Leaving aside for the moment the consideration of the peculiarly religious aspects of pastoral counseling, we may say that the task of the pastoral counselor, like that of the psychotherapist, is conditioned in decisive ways not only by the social system within which he finds himself, but also by the strains within that system at a given period.

In simplest terms this means that the troubled person must be understood in relation to social class, occupation, local community integration or disintegration, the oversocialization of the middle class and the undersocialization of the lower-income groups, the training available within the society for achieving a sense of identity, differentiations in modal personalities, economic power and powerlessness,

209

majority-group or minority-group status, the viability or decay of a symbol system, and the existence of a variety of norms.

An enormous literature is accumulating regarding these phenomena and relationships. Obviously, the pastoral counselor who is even quasi-professional cannot be innocent of these relationships or of this literature. Seward Hiltner's Alden-Tuthill Lectures of 1966 may be taken as typical of the (all-too-few) studies relating pastoral counseling to the sociological factors mentioned here. In those lectures Hiltner gives an instructive description of the social matrix of the American suburb which largely determines the type of mental illness and suffering in this milieu: the limited perspectives and perceptions of the population, the "anonymous conformism," the (unwarranted) predisposition to regard practically all difficulties except physical illness as family problems; and the anachronism of suburbia in the developing city. He shows especially "what these peculiar pressures do to and about suffering." [19]

None of the studies of this sort presupposes that the pastoral counselor may substitute sociological analysis for awareness of the unique person before him or for personal confrontation and sympathy. But they do presuppose that it is insufficient for the pastoral counselor merely to exhibit sympathy with the troubled person. He is expected to recognize and deal with the parishioner in his total milieu. With the increase today of juvenile delinquency in suburbia, for example, the pastoral counselor becomes aware of deviant behavior as "a property of groups."

The pastoral counselor or the psychotherapist can readily be discouraged in face of the heavy demands upon his

[19] Seward Hiltner, "Troubled People in a Troubled World," *Princeton Seminary Bulletin* LIX (June, 1966), 54-78.

energy if the resources of the social sciences are to be exploited in any systematic fashion. It may be that more attention should be directed towards living, interdisciplinary dialogue. In this connection I mention here the Boston Marriage Study Association, a small organization of which I was a member some years ago. This group was initially formed by Prof. Carleton Beals of the Harvard Law School, and was made up of representatives of the professions concerned with the family—psychiatrists, lawyers, judges, social workers, professors, and clergymen. At the regular meetings of this group we discussed the basic literature which we had agreed to survey. The group also arrived at a consensus regarding matters which a clergyman should discuss in premarital counseling. We even drew up printed forms for the purpose of reporting "findings" gathered by the clerical members from specific counseling sessions.

Through these meetings it was possible for us all to achieve an understanding of each other's roles and perspectives, and also in emergency to call upon each other for assistance. Only through some such interplay of perspectives can the rationalism that Wennerstrom criticizes be corrected, or rationality and adequate sensitivity in the practice of pastoral care be approximated. By this means also one can make available the constant reminder that every personal problem is a social problem, and that every social problem is a personal problem.

Social Ethical Norms and Pastoral Care

We turn now, finally, to a still broader context of pastoral care in its relation to social ethics, consideration of the ethical norms that give structure to subjective and objective values.

211

Earlier in this chapter the nature of the professions has been adumbrated. The first criterion of a profession, we noted, is the obligation to transmit, criticize, transform, and apply the values that inhere in a cultural tradition. Historically, this element of the professional role has been symbolized by the academic gown, the sign that the professional man has been exposed to the disciplines of the humanities, the *litterae humaniores*, the study that aims to make one more human. Many of the professions today have reduced this obligation almost to the vanishing point. This reduction is the hazard of specialization. Neither the pastoral counselor nor the secular psychotherapist can properly escape this cultural obligation. Here "culture is another name for a design of motives directing the self outward toward those communal purposes in which alone the self can be realized and satisfied." [20] This design of motives necessarily comprises both the subjective and the objective values.

A marked tendency in pastoral care as well as in psychotherapy, alas, has been to concentrate attention upon the subjective values. This tendency is readily evident in definitions of mental health. Almost at random I select this definition from a professional manual: "A healthy person's response to life is without strain; his ambitions are within the scope of practical realization; he has a shrewd appreciation of his own strengths and weaknesses; he can be helpful, but can also accept aid. He is resilient in failure and level-headed in success. . . . His pattern of behavior has consistency so that he is 'true to himself.' " And so on. Generally speaking, I would say that this definition clearly belongs under the rubric of only subjective values—of (secular)

[20] Philip Rieff, *The Triumph of the Therapeutic: Uses of Faith After Freud* (New York: Harper & Row, 1966), p. 4.

pietism. The orientation is completely noninstitutional. The conception of therapy here presupposed is apparently the notion that the therapist will assist the client to gain "the confidence needed to go forward to meet whatever the future has in store for him." [21] But for the client (and for the therapist) the future is bound to have more in store than merely personal problems.

The psychotherapist who fulfills his cultural obligation cannot confine himself to the task of promoting mental health as defined above. As a professional man he is the representative of the culture and of the critical stance in face of the culture. The culture includes the institutions and a criticism of them. Mental health includes the capacity to challenge the prevailing standards and to participate in their transformation. If this is not presupposed, then the above-quoted definition of mental health can become merely the recipe for "adjustment." For lack of space and at the risk of sounding quite dogmatic I venture to say that if a reasonable degree of maturity is the goal of therapy, the psychotherapist should look toward bringing the client into creative and critical participation in those social processes and in those institutions that constitute the public domain. He should aim to prepare the client to help change the society from which he comes and to which he returns. Any lesser aim can lead to social irresponsibility.

If we think of politics in this connection, can we not say that the old-fashioned system that places the client on the

[21] Barbara Wootton, *Social Science and Social Pathology* (London: George Allen and Unwin, 1959), p. 331. Lady Wootton's whole book is devoted to a discussion of the inadequacy of concern merely for the subjective values. She points out the undesirable consequences that follow from "reluctance to examine the imperfections of our institutions as thoroughly as we examine the faults, failings or misfortunes of individuals" (p. 330).

couch is in the end unsatisfactory? Ultimately, the client expects to see in the therapist an example of maturity in the democratic society. If the therapist is himself a political eunuch, if he is "not involved" in the processes that somehow affect public policy, he is himself an alienated person, immature, or mentally deficient (if not ill). And if the client is simply put back on the road to which he is accustomed, he may simply be restored to peace of mind in an organized form of alienation. From his therapy he may have secured only the analogue of what he would get if a revivalist were his therapist. Actually, he may not have gained the confidence needed to go forward to meet whatever the future has in store for him. The future might require, for example, that he come to terms with black power or with class-bound demands for law and order or with war.

The condition of the inadequate psychotherapist today is similar to that of the practitioner of medicine who is cut off from the rest of society. In face of this condition Oliver Cope, professor of surgery at Harvard Medical School, has recently argued for the inclusion of psychiatry and the behavioral sciences, anthropology and sociology, as important parts of medical education. He holds that the doctor today who is ignorant in these areas is not only intellectually (and probably emotionally as well) cut off from the world around him, but also ignorant in the practice of his own healing profession.[22] What is demanded here of the physi-

[22] Eliot Fremont-Smith. Review of Oliver Cope, *Man, Mind and Medicine* (Philadelphia: J. B. Lippincott, 1968), in *The New York Times*, August 9, 1968, p. 37. A similar view with respect to psychotherapy is set forth in Matthew P. Dumont, *The Absurd Healer: Perspectives of a Community Psychiatrist* (New York: Science House, 1968). See also the new magazine *Psychiatry and Social Science Review*.

214

cian is even more pertinent for the psychotherapist because of the scope of his therapy. The alienation of the psychotherapist from society not only distorts the intentioned therapy which he offers. It also induces alienation by reason of the unintentional, poor example he as a human being and a citizen provides for his client. A sophisticated existentialism should find in this truncated psychotherapy new material for "the literature of the absurd." Freud, with a different purpose in mind, has bequeathed the appropriate title: *The Future of an Illusion*.

One must acknowledge, however, that the traditional demand upon the professions to combine the general cultural function with the specialized theory and skill is a heavy one. The relative disappearance of the first of these functions in part reflects the conviction that it is too heavy. Few people would claim to know the solution to the problem. A hopeful sign, however, is to be seen in the reforms now taking place or being demanded in professional education; in medicine, business administration, pedagogy, and law. These reforms bespeak recognition of what Felix Frankfurter of the Supreme Court was wont to say, that the great professional men of the past century, for example, in law and medicine, were men who broke the mold. Wennerstrom's plea was itself a plea to the liberal clergy to break its regnant mold.

The reduction of the vocations of medicine and of psychotherapy gives us the paradigm of a widespread alienation promoted by the elimination of the first criterion of a profession, responsibility with respect to the basic cultural values. The reduction is in part the consequence of rationalism in the sense employed by Wennerstrom: addiction to thought-structures that are separated from reality. The drive towards rationality has produced a whole congeries of specializations that advance man's knowledge and yet in the process reduce the specialist to a torso. Max Weber has suggested that at the beginning of the modern era the adoption of a vocation was intended to be like the donning of a cloak. "But fate has decreed that the cloak should become an iron cage." [23] It would be appropriate to say also that in the professions the cage has been much reduced in size.

It may be said that the psychotherapist deals with mental illness of such acute quality that he can seldom hope to do more than assist the client to achieve or recover average interpersonal competence. One must acknowledge that this goal is not one that is easily to be reached. But if the matter is to be left there, we must then say that the pastoral counselor in a liberal church confronts a more comprehensive assignment.

The pastoral counselor represents, and is involved in, a community of faith. This community of faith presupposes that salvation is social as well as individual, and social in the sense that it entails response to the Lord of *history* and responsibility with respect to institutional as well as with respect to interpersonal patterns. Liberal Protestantism stands in the prophetic tradition that assumes that men are responsible not only for their individual interpersonal behavior but also for the character (and evils) of the institutions within which (and interstitially between which) interpersonal behavior appears. This is the pragmatic meaning of faith. This pragmatic meaning of faith is a meaning that is integrally related to the nature and mission of the church. Any pastoral counseling that does not function in the direction of this generalized conception of vocation can turn out to be the opiate of the pious.

[23] Max Weber, *The Protestant Ethic*, p. 181.

One must acknowledge that pastoral care, insofar as it has been influenced by pietism or by the narrow type of psychotherapy described above, has yielded to the temptation to reduce the conception of the religious-ethical mission of the church, and likewise has reduced the conception of the vocation of the individual member of the church. Reformism, as Wennerstrom says, may militate against the pastoral counselor's entering into therapeutic communion with the distressed person. But the remedy is not to eliminate reformism. One should not confuse a prerequisite of the therapeutic process with a way of life.

Actually, the type of pastoral care which concerns itself only with interpersonal, subjective values to the neglect of social-ethical, institutional demands is very easy to come by in the American church today, even though the minister has had clinical training in pastoral care. I recall that the late H. Richard Niebuhr, following his systematic study of American theological education, told me that, in the past decade or two, courses on pastoral counseling of the truncated variety had become so much of a fad that the study of Christian social ethics had suffered from marked neglect; and he added that the courses in pastoral counseling rather conspicuously neglected the consideration of the relation between pastoral counseling and social-institutional ethics. The consequence is the alienation of the church from the redemptive powers of God in history.

It must be granted—indeed it must be emphasized—that these redemptive powers work against massive demonic obstacles in a technological society and in a society riven with racial tensions. This means that the identification of the enemy is not achieved by the conventional definition of mental health or of pastoral care. The truncated definition of mental health can be a recipe for alienation in the guise

217

of therapy. Confining attention to subjective values and to demonic possession in the individual, it can by default give aid to demonic possession in the society.

Augustine lived in an age like ours, and in face of pervasive disruption he extended the concept of demonic possession from the realm of the personal to the realm of the cultural and institutional. Having been for years a professor of rhetoric and drama, he projected the protagonist and the antagonist of the play to the world stage, to the struggle of the Two Cities. At the end of the nineteenth century the elder Blumhardt in Germany revived an interest in the concept of the demonic as it appears in the New Testament stories of healing. In face of the impending crisis of capitalism his son, also a German Lutheran pastor, extended the concept of the demonic, as did Augustine, to the cultural, economic-political realm. Jesus himself effected a similar extension, a broadening and deepening of the idea of the redemptive power of God, by relating his healing activities to the wider struggle of the inbreaking Kingdom.

I recall from my experience as minister of a local church an incident that brought home to me the broad span of the struggle between the powers of the world and the powers that conquer the world; also of the struggle between "moral man and immoral society."

A member of my parish, a successful businessman, caught in the vise of the depression, attempted without success to commit suicide. In my conversations with him his persistent question was, "Why shouldn't I have done it? My responsibility to my family was taken care of by the insurance. I am nothing but a burden to them and to myself."

I could make no headway in responding to his question, and in search of aid I called on Richard C. Cabot of Harvard. Cabot pointed out that this man had a faulty notion of responsibility, for he had overlooked the fact that every time a person commits suicide he makes it more difficult for other people in distress to resist the temptation. This argument impressed the parishioner as well as me. But then the discussion came to the social issue, the meaning of the depression and the possible ways out. Pastoral psychology had to be supplemented by pastoral sociology, and also by the theology of culture.

Carl Wennerstrom says of William Ellery Channing that he was a man of "great soaring thoughts," but that he was embarrassed and frustrated in confronting the individual in distress, and that Theodore Parker was "a man of personal warmth, . . . always ready to help persons from any walk of life" and imbued with "concrete concern for them." This difference between Channing and Parker may have been largely a matter of temperament. In any event, Parker in the book cited by Wennerstrom made the first analysis of its kind I know of in American literature, an analysis of the great institutional powers in the nation (the power of business, government, school, and church); and Channing, besides promoting rationality and social reform, was bold and courageous enough to set forth the unorthodox doctrine of Patripassianism, that God the Father suffered in the person of the Son for the redemption of man. It would seem that both of them "linked the concrete enounter with the larger dimensions of ministry."

The concrete encounter with suffering is doubtless the alpha of authentic pastoral care, but under the Lord of history it demands to be linked with the larger dimensions of ministry. The omega is the inbreaking of the Kingdom through the power of the Spirit that both comforts the sufferer and forms the redemptive community. I know of no more succinct statement of the thrust of Christian faith

219

in face of suffering and tragedy than that of Daniel Day Williams:

The Christian ideal of life envisions something higher than freedom from anguish, or invulnerability to its ravages. Its goal cannot be the perfectly adjusted self. In the world as it is, a caring love cannot but regard such a goal as intolerably self-centered. What does it mean to be completely adjusted and at peace in a world as riddled with injustice, with the cries of the hungry, with the great unsolved questions of human living as this? We see why in the end we cannot identify therapy for specific ills with salvation for the human spirit. To live in love means to accept the risks of life and its threats to "peace of mind." Certainly the Christian ministry to persons is concerned to relieve physical ills, anxieties, inner conflicts. But this relief of private burdens is to set the person free to assume more important and universal ones.[24]

Presupposed here is the conviction that the relief of "the more important and universal" burdens is indispensable for the reduction of the "personal burdens." Every personal problem is a social problem, and every social problem is a personal problem. Therefore, sociotherapy and psycho-therapy must advance together. Separated from each other, they yield something less than, indeed something other than, therapy.

Pastoral care, then, within the context of a community of faith, has the task of eliciting a sense of identity and vocation in a social world of tragedy and injustice, and in a world of new possibilities. These possibilities are mysteriously available to those who, under the Great Task-master's eye, are of contrite and venturesome spirit; but ultimately they are hidden within his hands.

[24] Daniel Day Williams, *The Minister and the Care of Souls* (New York: Harper & Row, 1961), pp. 25-26.

THE CONTRIBUTION OF LIBERALS TO PASTORAL CARE

Seward Hiltner

In the first chapter of this book Carl Wennerstrom described his dismay upon becoming involved in the modern pastoral care movement to find little being done about it by his fellow Unitarians. In a striking and original way he tried to locate the causes of this paradox. Liberals, with Unitarians on their left wing, ought to be the leaders in this movement. But as he saw it, the lead had been assumed by the churches and ministers of the center and right wing in Protestantism.

At the time Carl Wennerstrom began making his observations, in the early 1950's, and continuing until the present, his description is, I believe, generally accurate. The largest advances in clinical pastoral education and related modes of preparation for pastoral care have been made, since World War II, by Lutherans, Presbyterians, Episcopalians, Methodists, and Southern Baptists.

If Carl Wennerstrom had lived to complete his project, however, he would have had to examine the early days of the modern pastoral care movement,

221

beginning in the 1920's. There he would have seen what I shall set forth in this chapter; that, when correctly defined, liberals were the pioneers in modern pastoral care just as they were in the modern movement for Christian social ethics.

Even if I succeed in demonstrating this thesis, Carl Wennerstrom's basic argument will still stand, namely, that liberals in general and Unitarians in particular need to pay more attention to pastoral care. If it can be shown that some of them, not so long ago, did so, then additional force may be given to Carl Wennerstrom's deeply held conviction that pastoral care and social action should go together, and that there is grave danger when the liberal side is associated entirely with social action and separated from pastoral care.

Locating the Liberals

It is a truism that liberalisms are characterized by their spirit and attitude rather than by their content. The content must change with time and situation. What persists is the effort to cast off shackles. But every liberalism must have a content relevant to the chains of its time.

Protestant liberalism during the first third of this century was focused around two poles: the social-ethical and the theological.

For many years, but not recently, the key to liberalism on the social-ethical front was the "social gospel." Taking account of the new conditions brought about by industrialization and urbanization, it attempted, in the words of F. Ernest Johnson, to "synchronize individual and social redemption." [1] Johnson's careful reappraisal of this movement

[1] *The Social Gospel Re-Examined* (New York: Harper & Brothers, 1940), p. 26.

in 1940 shows it to have been often wrongly accused of belief in inevitable progress and man's inherent and unadulterated goodness. It did, Johnson admits, deal too lightly "with the tragic conflict that goes on in the will of man," and it gave too little attention to "the personal ground of social redemption." [2] What it was reaching for, however, was "an authoritative Christian social ethic," despite the fear and opposition of those who believed "that the evangelical message was being diluted." [3]

The so-called Social Creed of the Churches was set forth in 1908 at the time the Federal Council of the Churches of Christ in American was formed. The creed had to argue in favor of collective bargaining rights for workers, for the very principle of racial equality, and for other similar principles. By the time F. Ernest Johnson wrote *The Social Gospel Re-Examined* in 1940, virtually all these principles had been adopted not only by the United States as a government but also by the majority of its people. True, adoption of the principles does not quickly bring economic justice, racial equality, or freedom from war. But the achievement of the social gospel at the level of changed principles ought not too lightly to be set aside.

By the time I began my professional career in the early 1930's, both the economic depression and Reinhold Niebuhr had dealt body blows to the rather undue optimism that had crept into the social gospel movement. Many Christian liberals of the 1930's, like their secular counterparts, strove mightily but then became disillusioned when peace and justice did not at once reward their efforts. Disillusionment is the hazard of liberals; and those with weak social and

[2] *Ibid.*
[3] *Ibid.*, p. 1.

theological vistas succumbed. The majority, while no longer calling themselves by the then unpopular epithets of "liberal" or "social gospel" continued the search.

The other pole of Protestant liberalism during the first three decades of this century was theological. Much of the liberalizing was focused on understanding the Bible. The shackles were literal inerrancy of every word in the Bible, preoccupation with various forms of otherworldliness at the price of getting on with this world, and a kind of rigid commitment—whether doctrinal, liturgical, or personal-ethical—which enchained the mind and prevented the encounter of Christian insight with modern knowledge.

Both the symbol and the creative-if-reluctant leader of this movement to free the Bible and theology from old shackles was Harry Emerson Fosdick. The epithet for him and others, set forth by the opposition, was "modernist." In Fosdick the Bible showed the hand of God as before, but it showed it through real people, who were ambiguous and sinful as well as brave and devoted. The people of Israel were seen not as marble statues but as developing under the tutelage of God. The words of Scripture were seen first in their historical and developmental context. Literalism was set aside as nonhistorical and subversive of the real biblical message to our day.

This theological liberalism of our first three decades, especially in hands less great than those of Harry Emerson Fosdick, was sometimes so preoccupied with the shackles from which it had been released that it failed to take seriously the job of theological reconstruction. Having put otherworldliness in its place, for example, liberalism did not often go very deep in analyzing this-worldliness; and indeed, often conducted its funeral services with the same pagan tributes to immortality of the soul as before. It drifted into

224

tributes to good intentions. Its positive content was sometimes not much beyond sheer moralism. Liberalism, like Sun Yat Sen, who fought a long battle to free old China, was not so good in ruling when formal freedom had been won.

Those were, I think, the liberals of our first three decades. Even Reinhold Niebuhr, the most severe and competent critic of the liberals' weak points, was nonetheless one of them on both theological and social-ethical grounds. Rightly, he thought it heinous to talk of Jesus' beatitudes as if they were either possible or legal norms for human conduct. He was realistic about "power." But he accepted and used every freedom from enchainment that liberals had made possible. He saw correctly that getting rid of those shackles is not enough. The ambiguity of man's self-transcendence, he declared, is forever with us, in individual man or society. Our freedom or liberation is a fact of life; and the issue is: what do we do with it?

Those Liberals Appraised

Today, every Protestant, except for fundamentalists and quietists, owes an immense debt to the liberals of our first three decades. The Bible brings us the Word of God. It is not, in its words and stories, itself that Word. We confidently trust in the God who is father of our Lord Jesus Christ for our individual and collective futures, as we do now, and have done in the past; but we do not have fine-print clauses about either the perpetuation of individual self-consciousness or automatic kingdom of God in one generation.

We are not chained to the Bible, but we see it both as a historical record and as speaking to us today if we can get through the complexities and hear that message. We know that the person must be seen developmentally, and the world, historically. Perhaps above all, liberalism taught us not to let hope be swallowed up in despair. Hope is not certainty. Hope is trust that comes out a bit on the positive side in face of ambiguity.

I had my theological education from this kind of liberal in the early 1930's at the University of Chicago. Some of of my teachers were preoccupied with what they no longer had to believe in. Some took historicism and developmentalism to mean that we no longer needed a metaphysics. Others took "naturalism" as a substitute for "supernaturalism." Most of course were fully attentive all along to the uniqueness of the Christian revelation. But they were liberals. And if I had not had liberal instruction at that time, I suspect I should have bolted the ministry altogether.

These liberals had been emancipated, most of them from extreme conservatism of some kind. Both their social concerns and their theological interests were genuine, but had a "release" quality rather than joy. As I now see it, they were in process. Their enchainment had been so real that they could not actually rejoice at their freedom now although they tried. Nor could they go after the depths in a new way.

Liberals in Early Clinical Pastoral Education

Since the movement for clinical pastoral education was what initially made possible the new attention to pastoral care, we shall begin with it. We find at once that the first public advocate of the idea of this movement was a Unitarian medical doctor, Richard C. Cabot. Although none of the other early leaders was Unitarian, in my judgment

226

virtually all of them may be called liberals in the sense defined above.

In 1925 Richard C. Cabot published a widely read article in the *Survey Graphic*, requesting a "clinical year" for theological students. Having been engaged for many years in medical education, he had learned the value of professional experience under supervision, and he believed the clergy would profit from this too. His theory about what kind of clinical setting would be desirable emphasized almshouses, on the ground that the primary need was for sheltered students to have direct contact with real human suffering. As the movement actually developed, almshouses played virtually no part in it; and Cabot, in his later years, focused on general hospitals as the preferred training center. Cabot, having supported the experimental chaplaincy work and teaching by Russell L. Dicks at the Massachusetts General Hospital from the early 1930's, joined with Dicks to publish, in 1936, *The Art of Ministering to the Sick*, [4] which has ever since been almost the Bible of this side of the movement.

Russell Dicks once told me of the period at Cabot's summer home on the Maine coast when a good deal of the book was written. Although he was then seventy years of age, Cabot interspersed hard work on the book with games of tennis and real swims in the icy-cold North Atlantic. Wealthy, successful, and Cabot though he was, Richard C. Cabot did some astonishing pioneering, and was very much a Unitarian in the sense of Carl Wennerstrom's covered wagons.

A specialist in diagnosis and on diseases of the heart, he was the founder of the clinical-pathological conferences,

[4] Richard C. Cabot and Russell L. Dicks, *The Art of Ministering to the Sick* (New York: The Macmillan Co., 1936).

in which a patient who has died is reviewed by a physician who has never seen the patient, and the checkup on the doctor's diagnosis and treatment recommendations are provided by the autopsy findings. When Cabot proposed such a plan in the early years of the century, many physicians objected, on the ground that patients might lose confidence in their doctors when they found the doctors could be wrong. A good thing, Cabot replied. His conferences proved to be of great importance for the continuing education of physicians, and by now are being imitated all over the world.

Cabot pioneered in other things. He was behind the movement for medical social work, and got it going first at his own hospital. He pioneered in the ethical aspects of medicine, and for a time taught ethics at Harvard. He wrote several semipopular books relating medicine and ethics, and spots of morals and religion, to the interests of the intelligent lay reader.

There was a period, about the time of the first World War, when Cabot parted company with the American Medical Association. Rich and patrician he might be, but he allowed nothing to stand in the way of the best medical practice and the fostering of ways to improve it. He was austere except when patients or friends saw him alone. On moral matters he was uncompromising and indeed absolutistic, his favorite theme being honesty.

When the Council for Clinical Training was formed in 1930, Richard C. Cabot became its first president. His interest in this body waned in the next years, because most of the training centers being established were in mental hospitals, and Cabot never accepted the psychodynamic understandings of much mental illness. I well recall the late summer of 1934, when the Council had its first conference open to the public. This was held at Union Theological

228

Seminary in New York. Most of us knew that Cabot's wife was very ill; and were not surprised, as the sessions opened, to hear that she had just died and that Cabot's appearance that evening to give the major address was problematical. Within a short time, however, a second message arrived. Cabot would be present. And he was. He had done all that he could for his wife. It would be a couple of days before the funeral. Why should he not get on with his commitments? I can recall the awe that went through all of us at this evidence of psychic strength. At this point perhaps above all others, I think Richard C. Cabot was a Unitarian and a New Englander at the same time.

In the last half of the 1930's, Cabot joined the faculty of the Andover Newton Theological School, where the clinical education movement had been introduced by A. Philip Guiles. They were especially concerned to expand this movement to other general hospitals, and did so. When the Institute of Pastoral Care was born in the early 1940's, its initial education was entirely in general hospitals. Later on, it expanded and also included mental hospitals as sites for training. Through the 1940's the group in the Boston area concerned with clinical pastoral education was larger than anywhere else; and for purposes of discussing issues and ideas, they banded together as the "Cabot Club." Through the continuing Cabot Trust, some of the educational activities are still being supported financially by Richard C. Cabot.

While editing this book and especially Carl Wennerstrom's own chapters in it, I have reflected many times on what might have happened in his retrospective encounter with Richard C. Cabot if he had lived to complete the project. So far as I know, Wennerstrom was the first Unitarian minister to follow the general course Cabot had recommended. He became chaplain of a great general hospital, and he did the advanced study needed to qualify for a higher degree. I am sure that Cabot's uncompromising position on ethical issues would not have been compatible to Wennerstrom. But had he studied more about Cabot, I think Wennerstrom would have seen that here, in the movement to which he was committed, there were the covered wagons, and that Unitarians might well take a bit of credit for them.

The greatest leader of the movement for clinical pastoral education was Anton T. Boisen, who died only recently at the age of eighty-nine. Boisen told his own story better than any one else can do.[5] Reared by the cultured and intelligent family of a teacher at the University of Indiana, Boisen had first been a teacher of languages; then an early graduate of the Yale School of Forestry; and had then attended Union Theological Seminary in New York. After service in local churches and overseas during the first World War, he worked for the Interchurch World Movement, itself a liberal enterprise of its day.

He was then stricken with a severe form of mental illness, and was hospitalized in one of the state hospitals of Massachusetts. In those days there was not much treatment in the modern sense. As Boisen was in process of spontaneous recovery after several months, he developed what was to become his central thesis from then on: that he had suffered a severe and undoubted mental illness, but that these very processes had also led him to new levels of depth in religious experience. Not that all religious experience need be like this, but that in himself and some others, the processes are the same in mental illness and religious experience.

Upon his discharge from the hospital, Boisen determined to study whatever he could that would help, to try to get

[5] *Out of the Depths* (New York: Harper & Row, 1960).

a post as chaplain of a mental hospital, and to bring small groups of theological students to study with him so that they could see the "problems of sin and salvation" in "living human documents" and not solely on library shelves. He found some teachers in the Boston area, notably Charles MacFie Campbell, M.D., of Harvard. In 1924 he proposed to Doctor William A. Bryan, Superintendent of the Worcester State Hospital (not the one where Boisen had been ill) that he be employed as chaplain. His offer was accepted. Bryan was a bold spirit. As he subsequently explained, after the Boisen movement had proved its solidity, "I'd hire a horse doctor if I thought he could help my patients."

In 1925 Boisen brought the first group of theological students to Worcester to study with him. For their financial support and their contacts with mental illness, they worked a full day as attendants, and then had evening seminars with Boisen. Later the movement was of course to be able to have its ministers and theological students deal with patients in their proper professional role.

This is not the place to document the leading influence of Boisen upon the subsequent history of the clinical pastoral education movement. His twin contentions, at the educational level, were for contacts under supervision, and for theological reflection on the contacts. For a period during the 1940's, a good part of the movement gave too little attention to Boisen's theological interest. But happily, in the 1950's and today, this interest is serious and resurgent, although in a somewhat broader framework than Boisen's special concern.

I believe Boisen would not mind hearing me call him a theological liberal. Like any good liberal (as I have tried to define liberals), he was a trailblazer at considerable cost in energy, time, and money. Also like an honest liberal,

231

he felt himself to be within the tradition. He often said that he was as concerned as the most orthodox of our Christian ancestors about the basic matters of sin and salvation, and that what he had introduced into the theological curriculum was not new content but the "method" of studying living human documents.

The content of Boisen's own theology had a large admixture of late-nineteenth-century moralism, and he eventually wove into it a respectable interest in mysticism. But the entire spirit of his theological inquiry was precisely as liberal as that of his teacher at Union Theological Seminary, George A. Coe. Indeed, he shocked some vaunted liberals when he insisted on writing about Jesus' messianic consciousness in the light of psychopathology.

Cabot and Boisen were the titans of this movement in its early days. As very different as they were, both combined moral rigor with fearless exploration of frontiers. They had quite different theories about the clinical education of clergy, Cabot simply stressing supervised experience with suffering and Boisen offering the mental hospital as the laboratory for the human spirit in its deepest quandaries, but they agreed on the need for contact in the pastoral role with persons undergoing suffering and for theological reflection thereupon. Both were liberals, Boisen more clearly in line with the long Christian tradition and Cabot, more Emersonian and New Englandish.

If my space and my detailed knowledge permitted, I believe I could establish the liberalism, in the sense defined, of virtually all the other early leaders of the clinical pastoral education movement. Here I can merely mention a few of them without detailed argument. There was William S. Keller, M.D., an insightful and loyal member of the Protestant Episcopal Church, who brought a group of seminarians into his home in the summer of 1923, sent them out two by two to hospitals and clinics and courts during the day and held bull sessions with them at night. In the early to middle 1930's, Keller persuaded Joseph Fletcher to join him and direct this movement full-time. Fletcher was then, and has been to this day, the most compelling liberal advocate of marrying pastoral care and social action.[6] Thus, I believe we may say inferentially that William S. Keller was some kind of liberal.

A. Philip Guiles, who was so influential upon this movement in New England, and who became the first full-time theological professor who had been clinically educated, was also a liberal in the sense defined. Like Boisen, he wanted theological reflection on the clinical contacts; and indeed, he coined the term "clinical theology," which I could never accept for linguistic reasons but the intent of which is wholly in accord with my own views.

Others of the early leaders and supervisors in this movement were Donald C. Beatty, Carroll A. Wise, Alexander D. Dodd, Francis W. McPeek, Wayne L. Hunter, all clergymen, and Helen Flanders Dunbar, M.D. All had a concern for the theological tradition, but all believed in clinical education of the clergy, and thus drove covered wagons methodologically.

Dunbar, then a brilliant young psychiatrist soon to publish the psychosomatic classic, *Emotions and Bodily Changes*,[7] had been in Boisen's first student group at Worcester in 1925, just after being graduated from Union Theological Seminary and before going on to medical school. When

---

[6] See Fletcher's two recent books for demonstration of this interest: *Situation Ethics* (Philadelphia: Westminster Press, 1966); and *Moral Responsibility* (Philadelphia: Westminster Press, 1967).
[7] (New York: Columbia University Press, 1935).

the Council for Clinical Training was formed in 1930, she became its administrative director and continued in this post for nearly ten years. An Episcopalian both by affiliation and temperament, she was nevertheless a liberal in the sense defined here.

Since I became a clinical supervisor in 1934, and Executive Secretary of the Council for Clinical Training the year following, I suspect I should set convention aside and admit that I, too, was at that time very much a liberal. During my four years of graduate study at the University of Chicago, I had profited most from the social-historical method of theological study then widely in use there, in the hands of such teachers as Shailer Mathews, Shirley Jackson Case, William Warren Sweet, and, to some extent, John T. McNeill. My first impulse had been to throw over the tradition; but I had come back from that, partly through the clinical education I had in the summers, long before leaving Chicago. Indeed, I can recall Henry Nelson Wieman's once calling me a "conservative." At that time, I did not like the theologies of either Barth or Wieman. But I suspect my liberalism was shown rather less in my ideas than in my actions. For I went off to the post with the Council for Clinical Training exactly in the mood of Carl Wennerstrom's covered wagons, with an inadequate salary, a pioneering job, and an idealism which, happily, did not grow disillusioned. So I, too, was some kind of liberal.

My point has been, throughout this section on clinical pastoral education, that all the major early leaders were liberals in the sense defined, although every one of them had a serious interest in the tradition and in being theological. Their liberalism was shown above all in their willingness to espouse a method of education, and consequent methods of ministry, that might or might not be new to the tradition.

234

They felt they were following the goals of the tradition. But if it took new methods and new forms of thought to effect such programs, then approach them fearlessly, no matter what the personal cost. And all the early leaders, with the possible exception of Cabot, did pay a considerable price for their investment in this movement.

Other Early Leaders of Pastoral Care

During the early days of the clinical pastoral education movement, there were some competent allies who had come at the subject from a different experience but who held similar views about the need for pastoral care to take modern psychological wisdom into account. Happily, I studied with one of them, Charles T. Holman, at the University of Chicago. The knowledge and experience upon which he based *The Cure of Souls*[8] had emerged from a combination of his local church experience and his reading. His liberalism was shown especially in his advocating that pastors take seriously the new knowledge being made available by medicine, psychiatry, psychology, and social case work. Apart from that, and from his novel case analyses, he did not break new theoretical ground. But his sound and common-sense writing had a deservedly wide influence both in directing new attention to pastoral care and also in looking to the allied professions for some clues about it.

Karl R. Stolz's *Pastoral Psychology,*[9] while more academic and less insightful than Holman's work, was nevertheless another liberal contribution to pastoral care in the early 1930's. Even when Stolz did not always say the best thing, he managed never to say the wrong thing; and this balance

[8] (Chicago: The University of Chicago Press, 1932).
[9] (Nashville: Abingdon Press, 1932).

of treatment, like that of the more daring Holman, helped to prevent the new concern from becoming faddish.

During the latter 1920's and the 1930's at Union Theological Seminary in New York, Harrison S. Elliott attempted to pioneer in Christian Education with his right hand but gave his left hand to exploring "counseling." Whether owing to Elliott or Union or both, this concern to utilize modern insights for helping people within the church was not set under the category of pastoral care. But of course it belonged there and was eventually so organized. I owe to Harrison Elliott my first opportunity at seminary teaching. And nobody has ever denied his liberalism.

I become baffled when I consider the propriety of calling Gaines S. Dobbins some kind of liberal. In terms of theological content, Dobbins has always been a clearly orthodox but imaginative Baptist. And yet when I read the charter of the Southern Baptist Theological Seminary in Louisville, dating from the 1850's, I found it astonishingly antedating those aspects of modern liberalism that were for free inquiry. At any rate, conservative as he may be regarded in many senses, it was Dobbins who brought clinical pastoral education and a new look at pastoral care not only to the Southern Baptists but also to the American South generally. It was he who first saw the extraordinary talent of Wayne E. Oates and supported Oates both at the Seminary and in related clinical programs. From this methodological daring have come, in the subsequent years, solid pastoral care programs in all the Southern Baptist seminaries. I trust it will not mar the impeccable reputation of Gaines S. Dobbins if I call him a "methodological liberal."

Time would fail me to recall the names, much less the supporting deeds, of some of the other liberals, at least in a methodological sense, who first supported the new movement for pastoral care especially through clinical education and related classwork in the seminaries. At least three bishops of the Protestant Episcopal Church were influential: Angus Dun, Henry Wise Hobson, and Norman B. Nash. Among Presbyterians, the movement found real support from Samuel McCrea Cavert, Roswell P. Barnes, and Henry P. Van Dusen. Van Dusen has written intelligently about theological liberalism, and is thus not likely to be recreant if I call him a constructive liberal. He was also an active supporter of the very early clinical pastoral education movement. Cavert and Barnes were my old bosses at the Federal Council of Churches and always backed me to the hilt.

Methodists were a bit slow on the uptake, and I cannot recall any Methodist bishop seriously interested in this movement in its early stages. But Methodists are more liberal than otherwise, and this situation was probably due to the enormous administrative load carried by Methodist leaders. A critical point for this concern appeared in Methodism when in the early 1940's a chair was to be filled at Boston University, and Paul E. Johnson was chosen. Previously a scholar and teacher of the philosophy of religion, Johnson at once took some clinical training himself, and in all the ensuing years has been one of the nation's leaders in everything relating to pastoral care.[10] Whether or not Boston knew what it was getting, or was just lucky, will have to be determined through the eventual memoirs of Johnson.

The Lutherans came to the new pastoral care movement slowly, and only from the 1950's have they been deeply involved. A few of the early students in the clinical pastoral education movement were Lutherans, and some became

[10] Of Paul E Johnson's many books, see especially his *Psychology of Pastoral Care* (New York: Abingdon Press, 1953).

chaplains, like Henry H. Cassler, the pioneer in prison ministry. At least in a psychological sense, for a long period they were "orphans." Prominent Lutheran leaders tended to express mostly alarm about this movement.[11] But times have changed, and no denomination is now more persistently dedicated to the clinical education of its clergy. Even the Lutheran seminaries now usually have teachers who have had clinical training. But except for the individual pioneering Lutheran ministers, we can hardly call the Lutherans liberal at this point.

My argument in this section has been that a methodological liberalism—not wholly different from the covered wagons Carl Wennerstrom discerned among the Unitarians— was present in all the early leaders of the modern pastoral care movement. And, in most instances, these early leaders were also theological liberals in the sense defined. Not only did they eschew theological fundamentalism in its technical definition; they also believed that the message of the Christian revelation, and of the Bible in particular, had to be brought into encounter with modern knowledge no matter whence it came. As to their doctrines, most were entirely orthodox. But liberalism need not be in conflict with doctrinal orthodoxy so long as there is room to breathe and inquire. Without such liberalism, there could have been no movement of the kind we know today for pastoral care.

Liberals Today

Except among Unitarian Universalists, "liberal" has tended to become a bad word today. Even though the old heresy-hunting days may well be over in most of main-line

---

[11] Frederick H. Knubel, *Pastoral Counseling* (Philadelphia: Muhlenberg Press, 1952).

Protestantism, nevertheless you can call a good guy progressive, up-to-date, imaginative, insightful, attentive to the modern situation, and have his appreciation; but if you say he is a downright liberal, he will wonder if you are trying to cost him his job—unless he is a Unitarian!

With due respect to Unitarians, however, I wonder if Carl Wennerstrom's assumption (that many ministers and churches are a little bit liberal but that Unitarians are altogether liberal) is any longer tenable? Put aside the reluctance about the label. Who today is really liberal?

Thanks to the battles fought and won by our liberal ancestors earlier in the century, none of us, unless we belong to the Pike's Peak Orthodox Fire-Baptized True Jesus Christ Church or its various equivalents, has any longer to fight for a right to use all modern methods of biblical analysis and criticism, nor even for a right to state Christian doctrine in our own relevantly modern way. Further, even if we have our situational problems about racial segregation, therapeutic abortion, Vietnam, or "the pill," nobody tells us that, as Christian ministers, we are entirely on the wrong subject. My first point is that anyone, including nearly all of us, who uses these new freedoms must in historical honesty thank the liberals of the previous generation for the privilege. My second point is that the content of liberalism has changed its face, as it always does, and that the criterion of true liberalism remains not as being unorthodox but as being liberal and open about method.

In our present theological and social situation I believe we can identify the opposite of liberalism. It is, for instance, lumping all "communism" together as if it were the same everywhere, taking a stand about this alleged entity, and no doubt waving a flag or a cross over the mark. It is questioning whether any kind of modern knowledge has light

239

to shed on doctrines, all the way from justification by grace through faith to providence and election. It is surreptitious legalisms, as are now being used against so-called Christian situation ethics. It is the recrudescence of moralisms as in the sexual sphere, without considering the new knowledge about human sexual response. In pastoral care, it is sometimes resorting to "hints and helps" and even to "natural talent," and refusing to analyze the tough ones where we have failed. It is also, sometimes, a perfectionism that refuses to see a problem unless we are sure we can solve it in five minutes. These are the enemies of a liberal spirit.

I am inclined to believe that the findings of Milton Rokeach, about open- and closed-mindedness, are of peculiar relevance today in the identification of liberals.[12] Maybe most Unitarian ministers are genuinely open-minded, but there is nothing in Unitarianism that guarantees that all will be. Nor, even if Lutherans and Presbyterians and Episcopalians are supposed to hang on to tradition, is there anything to prevent their being open-minded. One may be dogmatic, in the pejorative use of that term, about almost anything. My hunch is that it was this kind of dogmatism, riding on the coattails of its ancestors and not necessarily making any new contribution, that worried Carl Wennerstrom about some current Unitarians. Even the liberal churches may get sot in their ways!

Every liberalism is likely to be costly. Indeed, if it is alleged at no cost, it is thereby suspect. Liberals today may be Unitarians or Lutherans or Episcopalians or Methodists or Baptists. But I refuse to give the accolade automatically to the Unitarians. Unitarians may be dogmatic defenders of a previous era, taking the benefits from their liberal predecessors but, in actual fact, risking nothing today.

[12] *The Open and Closed Mind* (New York: Basic Books, 1960).

You can tell a liberal by his attitude, an ex-liberal by his disillusionment, and one who never dared to be liberal by his clinging-vine tactics of assuming that everything important is at hand. The true liberal does not attack people, but evils and deficiencies. His vision is always greater than his indignation. By these fruits is he to be known.

The "Liberal" Churches

By the attitudinal standard, virtually all of our U.S. Protestant churches, and large sections of the Roman Catholic Church, are today attempting to be open-minded, attentive to tradition but taking modern knowledge into account, rethinking the ways in which they have understood this or that, and examining both the historical validity and the current communicability, and so on. Every such church is, I think, even if it is not entirely dominant within an organized body, a liberal church. If it is more concerned with shuffling off than with getting on, then liberalism gives way to iconoclasm or negativity. But whether the epithet be *au courant* or not, a church moving this way is liberal.

Seen in this way, I believe it is still the liberal churches who are spearheading the pastoral care movement. No matter whether we deal with Lutherans, Presbyterians, Methodists, Baptists, or Roman Catholics, the currents can be identified as liberal by their covered wagons and by their reflection on their "fruits."

Liberals (who are neither traitors nor rebels) are against legalisms, moralisms, dogmatisms, and perfectionisms. Loyal to their heritage, including whatever are its unique dimensions, they are nevertheless in favor of analyzing any teaching or doctrine, including the tools of modern scholarship such as linguistic, historical, psychological, or sociological. Hopefully not captives of science, they nevertheless affirm anything that inquiry by scientific means can discover. They are suspicious, in fields like pastoral care and social action, of declarations of principle and consequent actions that are not subject to analysis of both subject and situation. Call them what you like. I think they are liberals.

Liberals and Pastoral Care

I have never been a Unitarian but I have been close. When I had an enforced tour of duty as Acting Dean of the Federated Theological Faculty at the University of Chicago, I happened also to be, for the year, academic head of Meadville Theological School. In the early 1950's when the Harvard Divinity School was trying to decide whether to perk up or go on the rocks, I was named to the committee to visit the Divinity School. Although Harvard, of Unitarian background which it is now trying hard to conceal, took none of the committee's advice, my service did get me acquainted with the great recent leader of Unitarianism, Frederick M. Eliot. He pleased me when the word got back to me through the grapevine that Eliot had said, "Hiltner is a liberal." It is true that I felt, and still feel, that the Harvard Divinity School ought not to sweep its Unitarian heritage under the rug, but should reexamine it critically and constructively. But except for my coeditor, James Luther Adams (and three or four others), under the rug it has been.

From my perspective the question raised by Carl Wennerstrom's thesis is not whether liberals and the liberal churches are carrying the ball on pastoral care. Nor is the question whether pastoral care and social action can go hand in hand; in my observation, even if you do not always have the same people pioneering, you have the same groups and the same churches. The issue is rather whether Unitarian Universalists are liberals on both fronts. If they set one front against the other, then they subvert their own liberalism. I believe this is a later way of saying what Carl Wennerstrom was getting at. How *liberal* are the Unitarians?

Nobody but Unitarian Universalists can answer this question. But I submit to them that the essence of liberalism, whether seen theologically, about social action, or in relation to pastoral care, does not automatically rest with them. They may be liberals or they may be dogmatists. Being Unitarians does not guarantee the one nor forestall the other.

As a Presbyterian, I think the Church Universal desperately needs Unitarians, whether they get admitted to the World Council of Churches or not. Without a left-wing witness of complete covered-wagon courage, Christian faith in general and our own focal concern, pastoral care in particular, may fall into some kind of "business as usual."

The modern movement for pastoral care was a product of liberals, in my judgment. They were liberals and not heretics, rebels, and backsliders. They kept firmly in mind the heritage from which they came. But they dared and risked, as any liberal must do, to get rid of the shackles and get on toward the goal. Today, liberals, and liberal churches, are found in many strange places. May I suggest that Unitarians take another look at the two great Unitarian contributors to pastoral care in this century, Richard C. Cabot and Carl Wennerstrom; and realize, in doing so, that both men, however different, were equally for social action? No true liberal can choose between those. Only defensive and pseudo liberals can ignore either one.

CONTRIBUTORS   *James Luther Adams*, S.T.B., A.M., Ph.D., D.D., Theol.D., has just retired as professor of Christian ethics at the Divinity School of Harvard University, and has assumed a similar chair at Andover Newton Theological School. In a previous post on the Federated Theological Faculty of the University of Chicago, he was first teacher and then colleague of Carl E. Wennerstrom. He is a Unitarian minister.

Anonymous is an able and distinguished Unitarian Universalist minister. He was interviewed by Carl E. Wennerstrom, later read the transcribed account of this interview and the analysis of it done by Seward Hiltner, and then wrote the "Response and Rebuttal" that appears as a chapter in this book.

245

John F. Hayward, B.D., Ph.D., D.D., an ordained Unitarian minister, is professor of philosophy and Religious Studies Director at Southern Illinois University, Carbondale, Illinois. For some years he was a member of the Federated Theological Faculty of the University of Chicago and then of the Meadville Theological School. He was first a teacher and then a colleague of Carl E. Wennerstrom.

Seward Hiltner, Ph.D., D.D., is professor of theology and personality at Princeton Theological Seminary and Edward F. Gallahue Consultant to the Menninger Foundation. During the fifties at the University of Chicago he served as principal adviser to Carl E. Wennerstrom in the latter's doctoral study. He is a minister of the United Presbyterian Church.

Harry C. Meserve, B.D., D.D., is minister of the Grosse Pointe Unitarian Church, Grosse Pointe, Michigan, and is editor of the *Journal of Religion and Health*, published by the Academy of Religion and Mental Health. For several years he was director of program of the Academy. He is a Unitarian minister.

Charles R. Stinnette, B.D., Ph.D., is professor of pastoral theology and psychiatry at the University of Chicago. He was previously at Union Theological Seminary in New York. During the later days of Carl E. Wennerstrom's doctoral studies, Charles Stinnette was his principal adviser. He is a priest of the Episcopal Church.

Carl E. Wennerstrom, B.D., was on the faculty of the Meadville Theological School at the time of his death in 1963. For some years previously, he had been chaplain of the

246

University of Chicago hospitals and clinics, and a member of the Federated Theological Faculty of that University. Originally a Methodist, he served a two-point Methodist charge while in college. In 1948 he joined the (Unitarian) Church of the Larger Fellowship, and in 1950, the First Unitarian Church of Chicago. He was an ordained Unitarian minister.

INDEX

249

253